"One of the best books I've seen that g[...]  [...]
regarding who they are and becomi[...]
Every woman in the world needs the [...]

SUSIE SHELLENBERGER, *editor,* SUSIE Ma[...]

"Margot Starbuck . . . says what all of us are thinking and, with God obviously whispering in her ear, tells us what to do with it. A must-read for any woman of any age who has ever wrestled with her body image. And who hasn't?"

NANCY RUE, *author,* Everybody Tells Me to Be Myself but I Don't Know Who I Am

"Margot Starbuck navigates the complexities of self-image, appearance, our bodies and beauty with humor, insight and wisdom. Get ready to be both entertained and moved. You will be laughing out loud one moment, then suddenly challenged with biblical truths that will transform your thinking and inspire change. Reading *Unsqueezed* is a truly liberating experience."

ANN CAPPER, *R.D., C.D.N., nutrition editor, FINDINGbalance.com*

"*Unsqueezed* is now at the top of my list for books on food and body image issues. Margot writes with authenticity, heart and a thoroughly biblical understanding of how God designed us to understand the human body."

TRAVIS STEWART, *ministry relations,* Remuda Ranch Treatment Center

"Margot Starbuck reminds us of what's most important: being who God made us to be. That's a truth any young adult, woman or man struggling with body image will never forget."

MICHELLE LAROWE CONOVER, *2004 INA Nanny of the Year and author, Nanny to the Rescue! Series*

"Margot Starbuck is one unique cookie. And her countercultural message says you are too so ditch the 'culture's insane enslavement to physical beauty' and get on with getting okay with yourself, just the way you are. In a quirky, often funny, über real and refreshing, altogether unhomogenized voice she [argues] against valuing bodies for how they appear. *Unsqueezed* is unsettling. Even if you disagree on some of her points, she provokes thought. . . . Fantastic."

LINDSEY O'CONNOR, *author,* Moms Who Changed the World

"This is a book for real women who have real thighs, real pimples and real issues with accepting the bodies God gave them. Margot assures and reassures us of God's amazing love for us just the way we are. Couch pants, here I come!"

AMY NAPPA, *author,* Thirsty

LIKEWISE. *Go and do.*

A man comes across an ancient enemy, beaten and left for dead. He lifts the wounded man onto the back of a donkey and takes him to an inn to tend to the man's recovery. Jesus tells this story and instructs those who are listening to "go and do likewise."

Likewise books explore a compassionate, active faith lived out in real time. When we're skeptical about the status quo, Likewise books challenge us to create culture responsibly. When we're confused about who we are and what we're supposed to be doing, Likewise books help us listen for God's voice. When we're discouraged by the troubled world we've inherited, Likewise books encourage us to hold onto hope.

In this life we will face challenges that demand our response. Likewise books face those challenges with us so we can act on faith.

likewisebooks.com

Margot Starbuck

UNSQUEEZED

Springing free from

skinny jeans,

nose jobs,

highlights

and stilettos

Bonnie—
You are God's
[STRONG] beloved!
Margot Starbuck

≋ **IVP Books**

An imprint of InterVarsity Press
Downers Grove, Illinois

InterVarsity Press
P.O. Box 1400, Downers Grove, IL 60515-1426
World Wide Web: www.ivpress.com
E-mail: email@ivpress.com

©2010 by Margot Starbuck

All rights reserved. No part of this book may be reproduced in any form without written permission from InterVarsity Press.

InterVarsity Press® is the book-publishing division of InterVarsity Christian Fellowship/USA®, a movement of students and faculty active on campus at hundreds of universities, colleges and schools of nursing in the United States of America, and a member movement of the International Fellowship of Evangelical Students. For information about local and regional activities, write Public Relations Dept., InterVarsity Christian Fellowship/USA, 6400 Schroeder Rd., P.O. Box 7895, Madison, WI 53707-7895, or visit the IVCF website at <www.intervarsity.org>.

All Scripture quotations, unless otherwise indicated, are taken from the Holy Bible, New International Version®. NIV®. *Copyright ©1973, 1978, 1984 by International Bible Society. Used by permission of Zondervan Publishing House. All rights reserved.*

Design: Cindy Kiple

Cover images: red high-heel shoe: 7nuit/iStockphoto
woman with umbrella: Haley E. Allen/Getty Images
Interior images: iStockphoto

ISBN 978-0-8308-3616-1

Printed in the United States of America ∞

 InterVarsity Press is committed to protecting the environment and to the responsible use of natural resources. As a member of Green Press Initiative we use recycled paper whenever possible. To learn more about the Green Press Initiative, visit <www. greenpressinitiative.org>.

Library of Congress Cataloging-in-Publication Data

Starbuck, Margot, 1969-
    Unsqueezed: springing free from skinny jeans, nose jobs,
highlights, and stilettos/Margot Starbuck.
        p. cm.
    ISBN 078-0-8308-3616-1 (pbk.: alk. paper)
    1. Christian women—Religious life. 2. Body image in
women—Religious aspects—Christianity. I. Title.
    BV4527.S732 2010
    248.8'43—dc22

                                                    2010008332

P	18	17	16	15	14	13	12	11	10	9	8	7	6	5	4	3	2	1
Y	25	24	23	22	21	20	19	18	17	16	15	14	13	12	11	10		

*For Zoë, who is **altogether** lovely exactly as she **is**.*

CONTENTS

PART TWO: The Purpose

Despite being naturally tempted toward the pinch of self-preoccupation, we were made for relationship with others

PART THREE: The Plan

We're set free from a binding preoccupation with self as we choose relationship with God and others

INTRODUCTION

A Third Way

Enlightened women like us *know* better.

After all, we're *aware* of our culture's distorted perception of beauty. We've been assured that the digitally enhanced models in women's fashion magazines have been carefully airbrushed to perfection. We've read that our favorite movie starlet spends six hours a day in the gym with her personal trainer, sustained only by a bare diet of cucumbers and water. We *understand* that Barbie's long, lean plastic proportions are not even humanly possible. Dissatisfied with our bodies, though—and against our better judgment—many of us still buy into it all.

The complicity of some, who look unnaturally fantastic, is apparent. This is not my personal situation. And although it will come as a pretty big surprise to most people who know me and the values I try to live out, on occasion I find myself trying hard to squeeze into the culture's hopelessly ill-fitting mold of beauty.

WONDERFUL
Strutting through an urban shopping district, the digital sounds

of Stevie Wonder piping into my head, I turn to catch a glimpse of myself in a storefront window. Though I pretend the glance is accidental, it isn't. I very much want to see how I look to others, while making it *appear* as though I have just accidentally flapped my head toward the expansive glass wall that I already know will display my full-length reflection.

Sweaty and overbundled, I'm frankly a little discomfited by what I see. My baggy gray exercise sweatshirt, accentuating my hips, is horribly unflattering. A few too many body parts are jiggling. My face is washed-out and pale. I look like the disastrous "before" woman on a triple-header evening of reality television: *What Not to Wear, Extreme Makeover* and *Crazy White Women Who Really Ought to Risk Skin Cancer to Darken Their Pasty Skin*.

Instinctively, I begin to calculate which aesthetic disappointments could possibly be corrected with just the right wardrobe, hair styling, makeup, rigorous fitness plan or cosmetic surgery. Though I have no plans to actually *do* any of these, I'm comforted by the thought that a few of the well-coifed ladies I see stepping out of fancy cars and ducking into restaurants could possibly, on a really bad day, look as unsavory as I do when they exercise.

Though I wish it weren't the case, these weird thoughts intrude regularly upon the satisfaction I would otherwise experience while listening to Stevie Wonder. Regularly, I spend actual energy imagining what would have to be done to me in order for someone to mistake me for a supermodel. The list, for those who don't know me, is quite extensive and more costly than I'd prefer to mention. Several of the body-altering procedures haven't even been invented yet.

The very spiritual part of me wants to be fine with the fact that no one has ever thought I might possibly be Tyra Banks's next protégé. When I'm honest, though, the part of me that desperately wants to be valued by a culture I don't even respect is a little put out. That part of me is wishing I were leaving a wake of crashing cars behind me because turned-head drivers, men and women, couldn't take their eyes off me.

To be dragged back and forth in a tug-of-war between the culture's values and the ones I claim to hold is absolutely exhausting.

> ## Author Disclaimer #1:
> ## Beautiful Christian Women
>
> **"If there's one thing I do *not* want to write,"** I told a friend emphatically over the phone, **"it's a book telling Christian women that they're beautiful. Yuck! Gross. Already been done. No way. Blech!"**
>
> No sooner had I said it than I realized: *Wait a minute, missy—that's what you do all the time. You love doing that thing! It's, like, your favorite thing in the world.*
>
> That's actually sort of true.
>
> When I speak to audiences of women, I do relish the privilege of announcing our inherent and undeniable worth as those created in God's image. I delight in declaring that we've been made for so much more than a death-dealing cosmetic preoccupation with ourselves. I love to look out across frosted, tinted, colored, permed, highlighted and straightened heads and see all the cartoony speech bubbles hovering over each one which announce, *Phew! What a relief.* Then, softening, the expressions on the faces seem to say, *That's really true, isn't it?*
>
> "Yes, it's true," I confirm.
>
> I really do love that great stuff.

OLDIE DAYS

I can't help but wonder if it was different in the olden days, back in the day when women were valued for their ability to reproduce. In societies with high infant-mortality rates and short life spans, fertile women were prized. The pages of the Old Testament paint a picture of this sort of culture, in which women with many children were considered "blessed" and those facing infertility were labeled "cursed."

These days, thankfully, we find that whole notion a little . . .
archaic. We look down our feminist noses at a patriarchal mi-
sogynist society that would value a woman based on her ability
to produce offspring. We breathe a sigh of knowing relief that
we've evolved so much in the intervening millennia that we're
not saddled with the kind of backward thinking about a woman's
value that links fertility to her worth as a human being. Sure,
we'll get a little excited if she squeezes out six or seven kids at a
time, but for the most part we're pleased with ourselves for not
placing an inordinate value on something so backward as prizing
a woman simply for what her body can do.

No. Instead, *we* value women with cut abs, taut thighs and firm
upper arms.

Rather than judging a woman on what her body can *do*, we
judge her worth on how her body *appears*. And though we absolutely despise the suggestion that we'd be so shallow to value
something as trivial as *appearances*, we do. In fact, our culture has
so thoroughly saturated our thinking that we value stuff like that
even when we don't want to. So while it's fantastic that we don't
officially pass judgment on women who don't bear children, I'm
just not sure we can be as smug about it as we'd like to be.

PICKLE

Most of us have in our minds images of the kind of body and face
that our culture accepts as beautiful. Though no one's handing
out a reference card listing the particular specs, most of us know
approximately what height, what weight, what shape, what eth-
nicity and what features are esteemed in our culture. (Hint: she's
a plastic, ten-inch-tall blonde bombshell.)

Unfortunately, for *Christian* women, our culture's obsession
with physical beauty is a double whammy. First we feel bad
when our muffin tops overflow the world's skinny mold—and
then, as people of faith, we feel guilty because we tried so hard
to cram ourselves into that death-dealing mold in the first place.

While women in our culture who don't claim to be followers of Jesus share our challenges around body image, they're not saddled with the extra layer of spiritual angst that Christian women are. They're not secretly ashamed that they spend more time on hair and makeup than they do reading Scripture or praying. They don't berate themselves for lacking the willpower to resist a chocolate chip cookie because disciples of Jesus are supposed to have enough power to cast out demons and move mountains. Women who aren't Christians don't live with a nagging sense of failure because they're more concerned about the cellulite on their thighs than the advancement of the gospel to remote people groups.

Christian women, longing to live a life in faithful obedience to God, find ourselves in a particular bind when it comes to our bodies. More often than not we're pulled like taffy between the culture's values and our Christian ones. Though we long for our lives to be formed and shaped and molded—transformed—into the image of God, we find ourselves more often squeezed by a culture that values and devalues us based on appearance. Longing to respond to God with our heart, soul, mind and strength, we're ashamed that we're losing the raging ground war against our inherent preoccupation with self.

Although we don't like to admit it, we *do* care how our butts look in blue jeans. We meticulously choose clothes that mask our unsightly bulges. We shudder at the dressing-room reflection of a body we wish were different, as we're squeezing it into a bathing suit in a size we swore we'd never wear. We fret, regularly, at the face staring back at us in the bathroom mirror. Some of us are ashamed that we do these things. Others don't even have the good sense to hide them. But even the ones of us who aren't particularly troubled by most of it can't avoid the fact that the time and energy and money we devote to the appearance of our bodies are, admittedly, inordinate.

We'd like to live differently.

SQUEEZE

Because so many of the "perfect" images we're fed by the media
are those of Caucasian women, I've sometimes wondered whether
women who look like me—a European mutt—are *more* likely
than some of our darker-skinned sisters to feel the squeeze of our
culture's obsession with a particular brand of physical attractiveness. I desperately want to imagine that it *might* be true. I want to
believe that the fact that people of color have for decades been
woefully underrepresented in magazines, on television, in film
and in all sorts of other prestigious places *finally* turns out to work
in everyone's favor—in this one slim instance. Unfortunately, this
just isn't the case. In fact, what we've got going now might even be
worse. In the absence of culturally appropriate drop-dead gorgeous role models promoting an unattainable standard of beauty,
women of color have been stuck with the mostly pale ones the
media has offered.

The results are painfully evident. Latina sisters are dying their
black hair blonde. Gorgeous dark Indian women are bleaching
their skin. Japanese women are having "blepharoplasties" to
make their eyes look more European. Noses too. Chinese women
are having their legs *broken* in leg-lengthening surgeries. Black
women are choosing makeup one shade lighter than their God-
given color. The state of things is still pretty disheartening.

One friend of mine happened to mention that more "substantial" black women *are* valued in black culture, by men in particular. For a split second, I was tickled about that great news—even
though I'm a married white woman who's not even on the market.
Before I could get overly thrilled, however, my friend wisely reminded me that this kind of valuing takes us back to the place we
didn't want to be in the first place: allowing others to assign our
value based on appearance.

Ugh.

I did file away that nice word—*substantial*—to enjoy by myself
later.

Before I'd even had a chance to enjoy it, though, another friend reminded me that the socioeconomic conditions contributing to a dangerous obesity epidemic among lower-income populations weren't really something to celebrate.

Ugh.

Author Disclaimer #2:
Body Image

I do not like the phrase *body image.*

I want to shy away from language that unnaturally separates the *body* from the entire person. Though the ancient Greeks clearly divvied up persons into mind, body and spirit, Jesus always treated people more holistically. In fact, he worked pretty hard to close that fissure, making the point on more than one occasion that restoring one's mind, healing her body and forgiving her sins were inextricably bound up with one another.

While we're on this, I'm not so fond of *image* either. Our culture's obsession with image is the genesis of the big mess in which women find themselves today. The fact that we've been conditioned to care as much about image as we do—to the exclusion of function and relationship—is a big part of the problem.

As might be expected, not wanting to distinguish *bodies* from the rest of our selves, and not wanting to focus on *image*—well, it really puts a wrench in things when you're trying to write a book about body image.

Thank you in advance for bearing with me.

That question about who we're really dolling ourselves up for is a critical one. I wish I were of the super-spiritual variety so I could say that I dress to please the Lord. I can't, of course. Nor do I think the Almighty even desires that odd thing. If I'm any indicator, for the most part we dress to please others and ourselves.

Many of us do enjoy attracting the admiring eye of both men and women. And the truth is that men, who seem to be hardwired toward visual stimulation, *do* take notice of the way women appear. And, as women, we *do* check out one another. Believe me, though the radical ascetic in me wants to say that appearances don't matter at all, the realist understands that they do.

The pickle in which we've found ourselves, though, is that too often we've given image more weight, more importance and more value than any of us are able to bear. This obsession with appearances has driven us to a binding preoccupation with ourselves. We need to be set free.

NEW WAY

We *realize* liberation as we embrace, with our bodies, the thing for which they were made: relationship. Can you even imagine a world in which the importance given to our appearance fades beside the shiny *real* purpose of our bodies, which is being in relationship with God and others? In this radical new world, mousy brown hair or dull black is just as fabulous as platinum blonde or shiny red. Skin that's pasty white and skin that's black as night and skin that's nondescriptly in-between are all valued. No one even notices the difference between flabby upper arms and firm muscley ones. Small flat breasts and big droopy ones are both completely fine. Same deal with butts. Whether or not someone has washboard abs or blinding white teeth or lean hips is entirely irrelevant.

In this alternate universe, the fashion situation is just as upside-down and confusing as all the perfectly acceptable bodies. Because clothes don't go in and out of style every three months, wearing the same coat for twenty years (when it hasn't fallen apart) is actually smiled upon. Scoring some cheap sweatshop bargain at the Stuffmart—in order to squirrel away more money to buy summer souvenirs at Disneyland—isn't nearly as fabulous as using one's extra resources to clothe others. People enjoy exercise together by walking between each other's homes for dinner, where rich and poor consume yummy calories together. Wouldn't that be the most wonderful world?

Great news, beloved! That's exactly the kind of kingdom Jesus ushered in.

TRUE BLESSEDNESS

Don't sweat it if it makes your head spin a bit. I'm pretty sure it was just as confounding for folks in Jesus' day as it is for us. In fact, one day during his ministry, Jesus weighed in on the way in which *his* culture valued bodies. He was teaching some crowds when a woman in the audience loudly shouted out something about his mama. I don't know about where you live, but in my neighborhood, those sorts of situations rarely end well.

What the woman in the crowd actually shouted out was, "Blessed is the womb that bore you and the breasts that nursed you!" (Luke 11:27 NRSV). I can only assume that that was some weird kind of ancient compliment.

At first I couldn't understand why she had to bring his mom's womb and breasts into it. Really, was that necessary? As I studied the passage more closely, though, the odd outburst sort of began to grow on me. In fact, I grew particularly fond of the King James translation: "Blessed is the womb that bare thee, and the paps which thou hast sucked!" (Luke 11:27 KJV). I really like those fun fancy words. In fact, I'm toying with yelling them out at my sons' soccer game this weekend.

Jesus, though, was no more willing to receive the compliment than either of my little soccer stars will be on Saturday. Nope. He didn't accept, and would not be defined by, the world's values. Jesus had no ostensible interest in endorsing a system of priorities that esteemed women for their bodies' utility in creating men. Even pretty fantastic men, apparently. Instead, Jesus redefined blessedness itself by responding to the loud fan, "Blessed rather are those who hear the word of God and obey it!" (Luke 11:28 NRSV).

You're not blessed, he's saying, because your feminine body parts work just fine; you are blessed when your body, your *whole* person, responds in obedience to God. That, says Jesus, is what really matters.

Go ahead, sit with that awhile. It really is as mind-blowing as you think it might be.

In a culture in which a woman's value was contingent upon her ability to produce and nurture offspring—which is, admittedly, a pretty amazing thing—Jesus placed an even *higher* value on perceiving and responding to God. He wasn't just saying that women are made for more than ancient prostitution, waitressing at Hooters or strutting down a catwalk. He actually went to the trouble of trumping something as fantastic as squeezing out another human being and feeding that offspring with milk from one's very own body. Responding to God, claims Jesus, is even better than *that*.

What was great news for first-century women, who were valued for what their bodies could do, is still great news for twenty-first-century ones, who are too often judged by how our bodies appear. In this new kingdom—a dimension more *real* than any of the lies that pass today as reality television—women who are infertile and those who are fertile, women who are mostly able-bodied and those who live with disabilities, ones who are eye-catching and ones who are not are called *blessed* when they respond to God.

Finally, bodies that are *blessed* are within reach of all.

1

LIES

Digital Fluff and Other
Modern Temptations

I had gotten all dolled up with mascara, lip gloss and my favorite green glasses. I was pretty excited to get my first professional headshot taken by Scott Faber, over on Ninth Street, here in Durham. Feeling very lovely, I carefully drove my car the nine blocks to Scott's studio so that I didn't sweat. I'm not proud about the driving, but it felt like a beauty emergency.

Before I went, I had imagined that I'd be a fabulous, fun customer with whom to work. I thought that maybe, after I left, Scott and his wife would remark to one another, "That wasn't work at all! We should probably even give her a discount. I hope she comes back soon!" In my mind, I would be *that* great to work with.

Only I wasn't.

I smiled tightly, self-consciously. Though I was absolutely desperate to appear carefree and lighthearted, I couldn't pull it off. Honestly, appearing relaxed is not as easy as some people make it look. Scott and his wife, Michelle, tried to loosen me up with their winning personalities, but I was still sort of . . . rigid. Thankfully, Scott took so many pictures I felt certain that one of them would have to work.

When the proofs arrived via email a few days later, I chose my favorite one to purchase. Once the money had changed accounts, I was sent the shot I'd chosen. Since I'm an artist, I opened up the image in Photoshop to determine its size. I just needed to know if it was bookmark size or billboard size. Once the file was open, though, I decided to crop it into a square. I'm a pretty big fan of squares.

Then, while I was looking at it, I found myself regretting that I hadn't had a mirror *right there*, in my hand, during the shoot so that I would have remembered to fluff my hair. It was just looking a little flat. Typically I'll fluff it if it falls in my eyes, but I've never been a big one for aesthetic fluffs. So it's really no wonder that I didn't think to fluff it, what with all the pressure to look relaxed.

Before I closed the file, I started to wonder what might happen if I just copied some of the hair that was already there and then pasted it on top of the old hair. I experimented with that little move and discovered what happens. Fluff is what happens. Digital fluff!

After a few more layers, I had that hair looking amazing. Hair model amazing, I believe. It was going to look great, I decided, on my website. That's where I advertise what I do. What I do, of course, is tell people, often women, the *truth* about who they are. I don't mean palm reader truth, but the truth that each one of us is entirely loved and accepted by God exactly as we are. That's sort of my big thing.

Isn't that kind of funny?

Let's Agree Right Now That These Things Are Crazy

1. *A nation with a frightening obesity rate coexists on the same small planet with millions who go hungry daily.*

2. *It is rare that I am hungry for more than one hour.*

3. *Today thousands of women will sit in traffic, burning precious natural resources, in order to drive to a gym where they will pay money to run, like a common classroom hamster, on a treadmill that's not even pointed at a window but at a television screen.*

4. *While many black adolescent girls eschew their full lips and dark skin, white women are paying thousands of dollars to have collagen injected into their skinny lips and are getting skin cancer trying to darken their skin both on the beach and at toxic tanning booths.*

5. *While looking online for books on women's bodies and self-acceptance, I was much more interested in the one with the lean, sexy belly on the cover than the one with the real, roundish belly.*

6. *Many of us pay actual money to drink carbonated, chemical beverages with no caloric or nutritional value.*

7. *This spring, as fashion experts dismiss last season's styles, affluent women will take their perfectly good clothing to Goodwill. Next spring, capricious profit-driven designers will bring* back *a variation of the old style to make more money off the same women who wouldn't be caught dead* inside *Goodwill.*

8. *Women with excessively large breasts, some who suffer horrible back pain, are going under the knife for reduction surgery, while women who* want *excessively large breasts are choosing to have them constructed cosmetically.*

9. *For a number of people like me, the need for more closet space seems like a bigger problem than the fact that we shop seasonally without ever actually needing new clothes.*

10. *I have to expend more energy and concerted effort to* not *overeat than I do to gather the daily resources I need to survive.*

FLUFFY FLASHBACK

All the energy that went into perfecting this image sort of took me off-guard. Over the years I prided myself on not caring too much about how I look. Anyone related to me can attest to this.

A number of years ago, I was visiting my grandparents at their home in New Castle, Indiana. During the trip I had decided to help them organize family photographs. The impressive collection actually spanned the entire twentieth century.

One of my favorites was a sepia studio portrait taken in 1941 of their growing family. My grandfather's jacket didn't quite close, my grandmother looks like a movie starlet, and my mother is just under a year old. The three of them had posed stiffly in front of a rich satin curtain—I imagine it might have been red if it weren't for the sepia.

As I studied the photo, I noticed that it appeared to have been altered in one spot. Looking more closely, I saw that someone had used a pencil to draw in some extra hair on top of my grandmother's head. It looked as if the idea had been to give the appearance of a higher lift to the tighter style that had been popular earlier in the century.

It wasn't hard to identify the culprit.

"Grandmother!" I barked. "I can't believe you *did* that!"

"Did what?" she asked, wide-eyed and innocent.

"You know *exactly* what you did, young lady," I scolded. "You drew on this picture to make it look like your hair was higher than it really was!"

"Do you really think I'd do that?" she demanded, sounding a little insulted.

Well, as a matter of fact, yes, I did. When she wouldn't fess up, I just kept working away.

Midway through the job, I took a break from my scrapbooking project to stretch my legs. I returned a few minutes later to find my grandmother hunched over the photo, clutching a black ballpoint pen and finishing the job.

She was so busted.

To this day I still have that photograph hanging on my living room wall, a reminder of the way this nonsense gets passed down through the generations. No one notices the extra fluff unless I point it out to them. Each time I do, though, I can't help but think of what she could have done with Photoshop.

CRAZY

I'm delighted to report that I finally came to my senses—with all the digital fluffing. I eventually chose to delete the fluffed file because, ultimately, it was lie. Oh sure, it wasn't a big whopper, like pasting my big head on Jada Pinkett Smith's nice little body would have been, but it was still a lie. Before what I'd done hit the tabloids and everyone found out about Fluffergate, I threw vanity to the wind and posted my unedited glamour shot. Feeling a little like a medieval monk, that's exactly what I did.

That Scott Faber is so talented, everyone *still* loved it. I got tons of comments on Facebook about how *amazing* the picture was. To this day, even with a new picture, I still do. Each time, though, what I hear in my head is, *That photograph looks* way *better than your regular face.*

I sort of deserve that.

2

SHAME

What's Particularly Devilish
About Hollywood Makeovers

When I was young, I remember sitting with my mom in front of the television set on Sunday nights to watch *The Wonderful World of Disney*. Today the Sunday evening show around which my family might gather is *Extreme Makeover: Home Edition*. In it, Ty Pennington and his crew of zany, warmhearted and physically attractive carpenters remodel a home for a family in need. My husband and children all love building, and I love the emotional drama and do-gooding. Family friendly, it works for us all.

Though few may remember the fact now, *Extreme Makeover: Home Edition* is actually a spin-off of ABC's original *Extreme Makeover*. In the original, an individual who had fallen into some manner of disrepair, or who had otherwise been deemed essentially unattractive by beauty professionals, was made over by fitness instructors, stylists and surgeons. Several other copycat shows quickly appeared on the network television evening lineup.

Though it was against my better judgment to watch these shows, like a sick voyeur I would occasionally linger.

I wouldn't allow my daughter, a toddler, to be anywhere in the vicinity of these train wrecks. I suppose that "mother bear" impulse might have served as a little red flag that perhaps I should not be in the vicinity either. I know that now.

My heart broke as I watched mothers leaving very young children to participate in these makeover extravaganzas. These extended absences, of course, were the only way for women to lose enough weight for family and friends and fiancés to drop their jaws in astonishment—which is great TV—at the final "reveal." Desperate children would then dutifully go and hug the skinny stranger everyone assured them was their mommy.

I never saw a child run away screaming after the curtain was pulled back, but I'm not convinced it didn't happen before the final edit.

TEEN VICTIMS
One of these horrible makeover shows featured teenaged victims.

I don't even know where to begin being horrified by this. I remember, in particular, one tortured girl from the Midwest. The moving melodramatic opening introduced the viewer to a self-conscious teen describing how her physical appearance—a receding chin, a crooked nose—had hindered both her self-esteem and her relationships.

I knew I should turn away, but part of me wanted to stay there and be furious. Fury trumped my better judgment.

"What is *wrong* with our society?" I asked my husband in self-righteous disgust as he breezed by.

What transpired before my eyes was as horrible as what happened in ancient Rome when crowds would hoot and holler as gladiators slaughtered animals, criminals and each other. At least in the coliseum there was no twisted pretense of *helping* the victims. I, though, imagined millions of viewers, at home on couches and La-Z-Boys, feeding off the teenage girl's misfortune and feeling a little happy that her life was going to, finally, turn out so great.

The heartbreaking message, to that girl and the millions exposed to the poisonous series, was that she was inherently unacceptable as she was. The deep suspicion with which she, and so many others, lived was confirmed not only by a panel of experts, but by the mother who loved her. Who would sign that consent form, I ask you!? Parents and professionals had met, conferred and agreed that the sinister voice inside this girl's head, hissing that there was something inherently wrong with her, was, in fact, accurate. It was true, they had decided together, that she was not acceptable as she was.

Though the show had been billed as the way to a *better life*—since they could hardly promote it as a twisted, twenty-first-century coliseum event—I couldn't help but suspect that all the delighted viewers, who were cheering on doctors and surgeons and trainers and stylists, were celebrating the death of a precious girl.

And possibly their own.

I absolutely hated the thought that other teens were watching that show. I know I should have hated the fact that *I* was watching it but, obviously, I was doing research. I wasn't as tenderhearted as young girls who were seeing another adolescent's "problem areas" poked, pricked and probed. I worried that when a cosmetic surgeon pointed to the irregular leaning of the teen's lateral incisor, the ones watching at home would silently run their tongues along their teeth, musing, *I really am a bigger mess than I thought I was.*

YOURS TRULY
The year in which all these makeover shows aired, I had just passed my thirtieth year. I, of course, thought all the teenagers looked fantastic. It was the thirtysomethings who were harder to stomach.

Typically, when I look in the mirror, I try to focus on the positive stuff. I learned this from my beloved grandmother. She taught me that if there's something I don't like about myself, I should never draw attention to it. Ever dutiful, I don't. I don't mention the body parts with which I'm not terribly satisfied. I barely even think about them.

If I don't like what I see in the mirror, I wiggle or fluff my hair, hoping I might look better in live action than staring straight ahead, frozen, trying to look like a magazine cover. I might pretend to be walking away and then whip my head around real quick, like a photographer is snapping a quick candid shot. Conveniently, the only real information to be gleaned in a glance that lasts a nanosecond is that I have a torso, head, arms and legs.

Satisfied, I can go on with my day.

This isn't at all how it works with the reality shows. Appearance professionals aren't the least bit interested in people who might be generally satisfied, if even in a squinty or whipping-head way, with the human bodies we inhabit. Honestly, even the participants who answered an online casting call on a whim, and who were sort of okay with how they looked but just a little curious and possibly wanting to be on television, will not be one bit satisfied after all the professionals have done their finger-pointing.

The dental surgeon points out a weird tooth irregularity. A hair-follicle expert highlights a thinning scalp. The fitness guru exposes flabby thighs and buttocks. A plastic surgeon yanks down on dangerously droopy breasts.

It's these surgeons who get me. Some poor woman who has five kids stands before them, naked, and they swoop broad circular markings around her abdomen with a fat red marker. The same red marker that looked so horrible and judging on third-grade spelling tests now looks even worse on postnatal bellies. I may be the slightest bit sensitive because this whole thing is my personal situation. If I'm honest, I'm not entirely convinced I *wouldn't* have a flabby abdomen had I *not* given birth. Since I do qualify to play the "I'm this way because I squeezed out a kid the size of a tricycle" card, I often do.

Here's the difference between me, raised by my grandmother to not draw undue attention to my faults, and these surgeons. I am very delicate with my "problem areas." Typically, I'm happy enough to just let them lead their own independent lives. The most attention my rolls and bulges get is the occasional pair of Spanx I'll squeeze into if I have to attend a wedding in a Lycra dress. Otherwise, I pull up my granny panties and leave these areas to their own devices.

Not these doctors. After circling the woman's belly mound—which would be humiliating enough—a surgeon will grab all the excess fat and skin he can lay his hands on. It's like that old "pinch an inch" commercial, only it is usually *way* more than an inch. When surgeons start grabbing at women's abdomens, I suddenly want to turn away in horror. I do not want to see the saggy mound of flesh that would otherwise stay under that woman's shirt and not bother me when she strolls by me in the grocery store. Squeezing her belly, the surgeon then says something like, "We need to get rid of *all* this." Dumbfounded, the woman nods in agreement. "Then," the surgeon continues, "we'll stitch you back up and you'll be able to get back into a string bikini." I'm pretty sure that what this doctor is doing has got to be a serious violation of the Hippocratic Oath. I can only assume that the promised bikini makes the whole sideshow spectacle worth it to the woman who has signed binding legal contracts confirming her willingness to put all of this weird stuff on national television.

What eventually happened to me, after watching enough of these shows, was that I started to think about my own middle. I didn't rush off to the bathroom mirror to expose it and grope at it and mark it in red, of course, but I certainly filed away the information that this gross deformity I'd just witnessed actually existed. On my very own person.

Hmmm, I mused the first time I saw one of those grabby doctors. *I didn't realize what a* mess *I am.*

I hadn't. But eventually, watching that weird postnatal situation get played out on television in my very own living room, I looked down to my lap and found the same big bulge.

Before that moment, I simply hadn't had the good sense to be repulsed by it.

How Shame Is Breaking Down Barriers of Ethnicity (or, The Nasty Lies That Women of All Hues Are Hearing)

1. *You're not quite right as you are.*

2. *Whatever you can do to fix yourself up is preferable to the way you were naturally made.*

3. *You ought to be pouring time, energy and money into changing your appearance.*

4. *Refusing the world's image of beauty can threaten your career.*[1]

5. *Attaining the right* image *is more important than being physically healthy.*

6. *Your mother really was right about all your aesthetic shortcomings.*

7. *All the expensive, time-consuming and self-obsessive ways you strive for physical attractiveness can be justified.*

8. *You need to disguise who you really are.*

9. *You're not free from the pressure to fit into the world's mold of physical beauty even in your own house of worship.*[2]

10. *You're not quite right as you are.*

---

[1]This one, though, may actually be true.
[2]Warning: this one could be true too.

YOU'RE NOT GOOD ENOUGH

What's fundamentally detrimental about these makeover shows is that, often, they are *making over* what God has made and called *good*. They evoke feelings of shame, in both victims and viewers, by insisting that we're not good enough as we are.

In order to sell advertisers airtime, these makeovers capitalize on my insecurities by conditioning me to believe the lie that I'm not acceptable as I am. It's a pretty easy lie to swallow. It's not a stretch for me to believe that God looked over all of creation and found most of it good, except for me and the squishy-bellied lady on TV. We learn our worth from the faces around us, and the face telling the woman on the TV that she's unacceptable whispers the same thing to my own heart. Though I'd love to be so psychologically evolved that it would just bounce right off my healthy self-esteem, I actually suck it all in like secondhand smoke.

I'm no surgeon general, but please: consider yourself warned. The danger of these procedures isn't limited to postsurgical complications at all. Lazy couch potatoes like me are also at terrible risk of inhaling secondhand madness.

3
MARKETING

Shame Sells, and
We're Buying It

Some folks might think this vicious cycle, in which the media and advertisers use shame to sell stuff, is new. Trust me, it's not.

During World War I, Listerine antiseptic, a compound invented in the late 1880s, was used to cleanse soldiers' wounds, saving countless lives. When the war ended, however, the makers of Listerine antiseptic, Lambert Brothers, abruptly lost the major market for their product. I suppose they could have gone around shooting people to drum up a little business, but that would have opened up a whole other can of worms.

The company finally came up with the idea of marketing Listerine as a remedy for halitosis. The only problem was that no one—save a few brainy chemists—yet knew what halitosis meant. Nonetheless, the makers of Listerine began splattering clever print ads in national women's magazines. Each one grabbed the reader's attention with a photograph of a perilous halitosis-related situation and a catchy headline such as, "Halitosis makes you unpopular," or "What's wrong with me, Mother?" or "Perhaps they say it behind your back." Then, in smaller print, the ads went on to describe, in soap opera fashion, what sort of pickle the featured woman had gotten herself into due to her unremedied halitosis.

In one ad, a woman is being shunned by men at a party. The catty friends of another woman, playing bridge, chat about her while she goes into her kitchen to bring them more salty snacks. During the decades in which women began to enter the work force, ads featured two kinds of women: happy and financially prosperous women who had *obviously* used Listerine, and the unfortunate souls with slipping sales who had not.

No one was spared the crippling sting of halitosis. In one particularly heart-rending ad, a little girl playing dress-up bride has been left on the church steps, sobbing, by a little groom-boy who told her she had halitosis. The ad continues on to point out how "lucky" Little Edna was to learn early what some people never learn at all. In another, an elderly woman who has returned home from church alone is thumbing through a photo album remembering the days, before halitosis, when she was surrounded and cared for by loved ones. I know you already get the idea, but each one of these dozens and dozens of ads is so wonderfully horrible that I can't stop myself.

Just one more. Brace yourself, because this one is particularly malevolent. The headline above a disheartened bridesmaid in 1923 reads simply, "Always a bridesmaid, never a bride." Yes, you read that right; this 1923 ad is the source of that sinister phrase. The reason the young woman featured has not married, the ad claims, is because there is something essentially flawed about her. The sinister hiss of the deceiver, playing on the deep, nagging fear in the heart of so many women, insists that we are essentially unacceptable; in this ad, it is being used to manipulate women to buy a breath freshener. It was so successful, in fact, that the ad has been included in *Ad Age's* ranking of the top one hundred advertising campaigns in human history.

The ads, of course, were created to sell products. Because they proved to be so effective at selling products, they were then replicated by other companies selling other products. In no time, the "embarrassing personal situation that can be prevented by using our product" schtick had caught on like wildfire.

The silent question of the human heart, which many will never dare to ask aloud—*am I acceptable?*—had been answered, definitely, with a resounding *no*.

In almost a century, not much has changed. Modern advertisers still raise a magnifying glass to our unsightly dandruff. They point out our ugly wet armpit stains. They remind us how unhappy we can be if we have frizzy hair. Or flat hair. Being doomed to a life of misery because of face wrinkles and cellulite just goes without saying. Advertisers work pretty hard to convince us that there's something fundamentally wrong with us that can be solved by the purchase of a product, service or fitness plan.

Most of us have bought it.

Ten Lies Advertisers Want You to Believe

1. *Your life will be better when you get thin. Just ask our spokesmodel.*

2. *People with whiter teeth are more attractive and valuable than those of us with yellowing chompers.*

3. *If you choose not to disguise any of the potential odors your body might emit, you're doomed for social failure.*

4. *If you're not wearing this season's hottest styles, you won't be noticed or valued.*

5. *The Fantasti-bra can perform miracles. Miracles you need.*

6. *Wrinkles and creases must be battled and eliminated, at all cost.*

7. *There's a big secret to weight loss that's easier than changing your diet and exercising.*

8. *Pit and leg and groin hair must be removed. Immediately. We can't say why. Don't ask questions.*

9. *Cellulite can and should be eliminated. Surgically, if necessary.*

10. *The particular product being hocked will actually* achieve *each of the above.*

EXPOSING THE SPLIT-END CONSPIRACY

As long as I've been alive, I've been fed by these kinds of advertisements, which insist that we're not okay as we are. The most absurd one, to me, is the one in which a woman with long, shiny hair notices that she has split ends. Her face falls as she realizes her predicament; the situation is dire. If only she had firm, unsplit hair ends, her life would be so much better. And sure enough, once she buys and uses the advertised product, she bounces and twirls and skips happily off into some otherwise hair-damaging scene, like a swimming pool. Since she used the product, though, we can all rest at night knowing that her hair will be just fine and that she will live happily ever after.

I wouldn't think that it needs to be mentioned, except that these weird melodramas still sell shampoo and conditioner and treatments and rejuvenators—with convincing graphic depictions showing the split-end molecules fusing back together into one strong piece of hair. Although the commercials have gotten us all pretty anxious about the splitting situation, these are *hair ends*, people. They don't even *do* anything. Companies have convinced us, though, that if our ends are split, we need to toughen them up. If hair is brown, it needs to be blonde. If it's kinky, we should straighten it. If it's straight, we should perm it.

It's not just hair. Advertisers have been able to convince us that just about every part of us, in its natural form, is flawed: our hair is too gray, too split, too straight or too kinky. Our features are too flat, too prominent, too thin or too thick. If our face isn't oily with acne, then it's creased with wrinkles. During the narrow window between *those* two tragic conditions, our skin is too dark or too light. Our upper arms are flabby. Our nails need polishing. Our breasts need lifting. Our stomachs need flattening. Our hips need slimming. Our buttocks need firming. Our body hairs need shaving. Our thighs need reducing.

It's time to say enough is enough. It's time to stand up and say, "My body, in its natural state, is good." It may not fit the world's standard of beauty, but it is *good*. When God made plants and animals and women and men, God looked at all that had been made and called it good. As is.

MY GIRL

I'm pretty serious about breaking this vicious shame cycle with my daughter. Part of my genius plan is to just put it all out there on the table. When Zoë was four, I asked her, "If there were one thing that I could change about you, what would it be? If I could make just one thing different about you, what do you think it might be?"

Fear and confusion flushed across her sweet round face. Tension escalated in her blood and mine. Wanting to please Mommy with the right answer to a question that was wrong, she dutifully groped for a reply. "Ummm . . . my hair? My eyes?"

Even though I knew I was setting her up, I couldn't take it for long. I let her search for a few moments, then jumped in to relieve my own anxiety as much as hers. "Nothing, Bird. There is *nothing* I would change about you. You are altogether lovely just as you are. You are *just* right."

Relief and delight burst forth in her big grin.

After the first painful round, I coached Zoë so that she'd be better prepared the next time we played the game. Now, six years later, she's a pro. Tucking her into bed I begin, "If there was one

thing . . ." I look for the predictable flash of recognition that lets
me know she's on to me. After the telltale eye-twinkle and broad,
knowing grin comes the sheepish and grateful, "Nothing."

I've been thinking that if we can just nip this thing in the bud,
she'll be freed up for much more important stuff.

Like living.

4

TEMPTATION

Even Jesus Was
Tempted by Carbs

While throwing back a mouthful of M&M's at the movies, one woman chuckles and remarks offhandedly, "I'm addicted to chocolate!"

Another, sipping a costly mocha latte in a chic coffee shop across town, confesses to a friend, "This is my only vice. I just can't start the day without it."

One woman, a cheese-lover, reaching for her seventh chunk, admits, "What can I say? I'm addicted! There are worse things, right?"

Though our socially acceptable addictions may cause heart damage, weight gain and other assorted maladies, we generally tolerate these. We smile nervously, knowingly. Even if it's not our particular vice of choice, we understand what it is to crave a particular food or drink that comforts the lonely, satisfies the hungry, vivifies the tired and soothes the anxious.

We get that.

At various times, this has been my personal situation. I'd either polish off a crate of Oreos or I'd refuse to screw the lid off a single one. At age eighteen I felt a little baffled and confused when a peer passed up an Oreo. She explained, "I realized that my body was addicted to sugar, so I just don't eat it anymore."

My reaction was a complicated mix of being at once disgusted, convicted, envious and very impressed. Because while it's a lot of fun to jest about being addicted to chocolate while scarfing some down, it's an entirely different matter to put it out there and then change one's behavior.

RATIONALIZATION

From my successful and failed attempts at fasting from cheese, chocolate and sweets, I now understand what my friend meant. I had avoided sweets and rich foods for about six months last year when, on Mother's Day, I decided that I sort of *deserved* to eat cheesy pizza. Obviously, with all the mothering I'd been doing, I'd earned it.

On the way home from that fantastic Costco indulgence, my evil husband stopped at a Krispy Kreme donut factory. The *factory*, people. This is where you get to peer through a big window at employees in hairnets making thousands of fatty donuts. Though I hadn't eaten a single sweet in six months, I must have been hopped up on some sort of happy-release from the cheese and was not making the best choices.

At first, my husband was a little surprised that I was going to join him and the kids in the donut indulgence.

"Well," I reasoned, "it is *breakfast* food." I feel certain I am not the first fat- and carb-starved dieter to use this rationale. "It's not like it's an actual dessert," I continued. "Now, if it were eight at night, then I might rightfully be accused of consuming dessert. But it's two in the afternoon, which is sort of a 'post-brunch' period of time."

"Yeah, before dinner is like breakfast," my naughty husband agreed. He's generous that way.

Though I'm not typically a big donut consumer, the fat-sugar combo sure hit the spot. It was also sort of the beginning of the end of my fantastic diet. Given the addictive quality of the fat and sugar, I mean. Rather than being truly *satisfying*—that is, the kind of satiation where you don't compulsively crave more—eating a little just made me want to eat more. And though I'm no science wiz, I am clear about the fact that wonderful magic happens in the brain, releasing happy chemicals, with the holy sugar-fat-salt trinity. It relieves anxiety. It causes happiness. It soothes feelings I don't even know I have.

Although I could probably, technically, make hunger disappear by eating an apple, cottage cheese or a healthy sandwich, the heavenly heart-attack trifecta clearly has a much larger purpose than hunger management.

Every time scientists release cutting-edge research revealing that the consumption of chocolate and cheese and donuts releases happy chemicals in the brain, I think quietly to myself, *Duh.*

TEMPTATION

The fourth chapter of Luke's Gospel describes Jesus' wilderness temptation by the devil. The first temptation the enemy put out there was asking hungry Jesus to turn a stone to bread. Is it really surprising that Satan started with carbs? That's just so predictable. Jesus' answer to all three schemes devised by the evil one was, "No thanks. I'll trust in what God provides."

Though it's a little tempting to spiritualize it and twist this principle into a best-selling diet book, that's not where I'm headed with this.

The conflict, the temptation, the struggle is one much larger than having the willpower to stick to a rigid Atkins diet. In fact, the enemy's offer to Eve in the garden, and the enemy's offer to Jesus, is the same one the deceiver hisses into our ears every day: "You don't have to trust God to meet your needs. Just take things into your own hands. Soothe yourself." With Eve and with Jesus and with us, I'm not talking about a physiological need for fruit or bread. I'm talking about the anxieties with which we live that we often *do* attempt to soothe with food and drink and shopping and staying busy.

And while some of us grab at the apple, or the apple fritter, others of us cleverly disguise the same impulse toward control, toward meeting our own needs, toward reducing our anxiety, by *not* reaching for God's good provision. We too fail to live into God's goodness as we purse our lips shut, clench our fists and reject all the other trees in the garden that God has called good.

Don't worry, this isn't some devilish trick to beat you up whether you reach for the apple pastry or politely decline it. Quite the opposite. As we unclench our grabby fists *and* our refusing ones, God's good gift is to give us what we really need.

Though some people imagine a red-faced Satan with pointy horns, a cape and a pitchfork, I think we're dealing with a much smoother cat than that. This guy's more like the well-dressed salesman who convinces us that he's got our best interests at heart. "Why depend on God to meet your needs?" the voice asks. "Why not meet your own needs?"

So that's what we do. We reach for a Snickers. A bottle of Scotch. A handful of pills. We control our environment by binging, purging, cutting or exercising excessively. We find all sorts of clever ways to manage our feelings.

I hear the same naughty voice that hissed in Eve's ear, and Jesus' ear, when I'm at the grocery store or standing in front of the open refrigerator or shopping at Marshalls. "Go on, Margot, reach for it. You don't have to depend on God for provision and comfort; you can soothe yourself." The next thing I know, I've done something I'll regret that involves Oreos, quesadillas or sequined purple tennis shoes.

Jesus' response, though, was different. Jesus—faced with the same physical and emotional hunger that gnaws at our own insides—chose to trust in what his Father, and ours, provides.

We hear Jesus reiterate that trust the night before he was cruci-fied. Kneeling in prayer, Jesus asks for the trial to be taken from him. "Father, if you are willing, take this cup from me." Then, ut-tering the words that I often do not mouth, Jesus adds, "yet not my will, but yours be done" (Luke 22:42). Jesus chose to trust in what the Father provides.

The next day, hanging on the cross, Jesus was offered a sponge with gall. Gall, an ancient drug, would have eased the pain that Christ was enduring. Jesus, though, who had refused illicit bread and who had received a bitter cup, refused the numbing drug. He refused to depend upon anything other than his Father.

Faced with hunger, fear and pain—just like we are—Jesus chose *against* relieving his own discomfort. Instead, he chose to endure the way that seems like death. He relinquished control by bravely trusting in what God provides, choosing instead to en-dure the way that feels like death.

DEATH WAY

It's uncanny how the way to life can often feel almost indistin-guishable from death.

Really, isn't that the reason some of us avoid deprivation in the first place? We reject self-denial, and we resist going cold turkey. We avoid withdrawal symptoms, caffeine cravings and bodily hunger because they feel like death. Given a choice, like Eve we'd much rather grasp at a quick fix—something to satisfy our needs, cravings and addictions—than trust that God will provide.

I get that. Believe me, I do. It's sort of the human way.

And while some of us reject deprivation, others of us groove on it. Though we may not overeat, or binge, or even bulge, the hypercontrol we exercise as we meticulously restrict calories, or carbs, or sweets can be equally death-dealing. For us, the stran-gling grip of self-denial has been squeezing the life right out of us. To even consider releasing that control feels like death. So while the Rubenesque idol of gluttony might be easier to spot on the freezer shelf or at the all-you-can-eat buffet, the grubby little statue of rigid self-control is hiding right behind her.

And yet the One who is the Way invites us into something altogether different. I don't mean a rigid, lawlike self-discipline. I don't mean that if we could all just whip up more trust in God to meet our needs that we'd kick all our bad habits. A critical God is not pointing a finger at the alcoholic, the addict, the chronic liar, the compulsive shopper, the sex addict or the overeater, demanding that we whip up enough self-control to resist temptation. God knows us better than that. God knows what makes us tick.

Instead, God quietly invites us to trust him.

I think God hangs out at hospitable churches on Friday nights, waiting for the Narcotics Anonymous crowd to arrive. As each humbled woman and man passes through the doors, for her first meeting or his forty-first one, the Father who loves each one quietly cheers, "Hang in there, baby. You can do it. I am *for* you."

I think God lingers on the stoop of the liquor store, ready to hop into the passenger seat of a car driven by an ambivalent alcoholic. "I know it feels like death to drive away empty," God whispers, "but it's the way. I'm with you, kid. I'm *for* you."

Beside every vending machine, grocery cashier and endless buffet, God urges the desperate eater, "You're not alone. I am *for* you. You can trust me with your deepest hunger. Although I know it doesn't feel like it, you *will* survive feeling even your deepest hurt."

Jogging next to every starved teenage girl, running her hungry self to death, the Father invites, "Let me give you rest. Taste and see that I am good. I am *for* you."

And although the enemy tries to convince us that depending on God is the way of death, and though it usually *feels* that way, it's really the Way to freedom. The same Spirit that sustained Jesus in the wilderness is gently wooing us to embrace this new Way, whispering to the ears of our hearts: "Trust me: you were made for more."

5

JUDGMENT

My Butt Is Ranwd

My son is in first grade. At my quarterly conference with his teacher, I got to see his science journal. Who even knew first graders *had* science? On page one he described the properties of a certain mystery object.

My object is white.
My object is ranwd.
My object is hard.
My object can sink.

After reading the first clue on his list, my initial guess was *piece of paper*. That's probably because he'd written on paper. Then, after the second hint about it being round, I thought the answer might be *marshmallow*. (I was hungry.) After the third one I was hoping it wasn't a marshmallow, because if it was, it would be a stale one. By the fourth clue, I was thinking *doorknob*. Finally, when I asked him, I found out that his object was a thin silver washer, the kind that I might easily lose off of my mountain bike while changing a tire.

By describing an object's properties, we figure out what it is.

We decide whether we should use it to fix a bicycle or whether we should melt it over a campfire for a tasty snack.

When we encounter a person, we do the same thing. Before we ever have a conversation with someone—before we find out if she's gracious or generous or compassionate—we notice her color, her shape, her size, her gender and her age.

This is one reason I think it's a little funny that, when it comes to race, some of us like to say we don't see color. More often than not it's white people who say this. While I'm not sure that's even possible unless one is a canine, I usually feel suspicious when people speak this way. I'd be equally dubious if someone claimed not to notice shape or size. If I'm feeling charitable, I'll assume that what they're *trying* to say is, "All men, and women too, were created equal." I understand that that's most likely the good intention.

Even if I am feeling charitable, though, I don't buy it for a second.

Of course we see color and shape and size. Every first grader knows that. Noticing isn't the problem. The thing that's shameful is when, based on her appearance, we assign a person a value that's either greater than or less than the one assigned to her by her Maker.

Right there: that's the problem.

Wanting to give everyone the benefit of the doubt, I want to believe that this keen attention to difference was once useful. I want to believe that the very survival of humans, clumped in homogenous little tribes, might have been naturally threatened by some band of outsiders who didn't match the tribe. I want to believe that whatever adrenaline shot through people's bodies when they saw someone different entering their cave or meadow or village was meant for their protection. I desperately want to believe that there's some good, ancient reason for this noticing, because these days there's usually no good reason for us to be alarmed or afraid about the differences we notice in others.

If only logical reasoning stopped us.

WE SEE SIZE

Aware of how tangled up most of us are about differences in size and shape and color because of our culture, I try really, really hard not to notice—until I can't *not* notice anymore. A woman could be eight feet tall, or four hundred pounds, or have pink hair or blue skin, and I'll just act like there is nothing at all out of the ordinary. The fact is that I should probably be more alarmed than I usually try not to be if I *did* meet a woman who was blue. I'm sure I'd be much more helpful to her, if by chance she was choking on something, than I would be when acting entirely unalarmed. You can see how it's all very complicated.

Last night I was sitting at the dinner table with my kids consuming calories, like families are supposed to do, when I found myself in one of these situations.

"Keith is small for his age," one remarked.

Keith, thirteen years old, is a close friend of the family. I don't even remember now which child mentioned it. I just remember panicking a little once it was out there.

I felt panicky because I'm so keenly aware that our culture places an inordinate value on slight, bony women and large, hulking men. I think I became anxious because I see neither of these as viable possibilities for a few of the children I love, of both genders, who were sitting at the table. This is why I panicked. Of course, as I scanned their faces for signs of judgment about Keith's size, I saw none. It just was what it was. My children are young enough that they're not quite as messed up as I am. Yet.

My first impulse was to say something to fill the silence of their not-judging. I couldn't help but feel a little proud that I *did* resist the temptation to corroborate God in the whole mess by saying, "God made Keith just the way he is!" While this is pretty much true, too often when we pit God against the allure of culture, it's the Holy One who's going to get the short end of the stick. Even if my kids embraced the idea now, a few years down the road God would end up getting blamed for acne, straight hair and other sundry difficulties.

The other temptation is always to play the "still growing" card. I also have just barely enough sense not to play that devilish joker. In fact, I've made it a personal policy never to offer a hollow "Well, he's still growing" in order to appease anyone feeling small. That's just playing into the whole sinister game. I'm not about to pin my hopes and dreams on the possibility that a small boy will bulk up into an NFL linebacker and a tall muscley girl will slim down and find her inner supermodel.

I suppose those things *could* happen, of course. If they did, I mused silently as my kids continued to force down their spinach leaves, if any one of my children *did* grow up to be exactly the right size and shape to fit into the world's rigid mold of attractiveness, I'd just pretend not to notice, like I do with pink and blue women. Yes, I decided with certainty, that's exactly what I'd do. I'd look deep into my child's eyes and bless his or her inner being without making admiring comments about how incredibly muscular he is or how deliriously trim she is. This whole brilliant plan came to me in the anxious, searching nanoseconds after one of them mentioned that Keith was small.

Praying my children wouldn't perceive all this crazy anxiety with which I live, I tried to look very calm and peaceful on the outside while, on the inside, I was desperately clawing for something meaningful to say about Keith's size.

Before I was able to spit out one word, my youngest, not much bigger than a field mouse himself, said, "I'm small for my age too."

He spoke it as if the information was the same variety of cereal-box factoid as "lizards have tails" or "cars have wheels."

The announcement surprised me a bit. Because, like so many of us, he has days when he's not entirely thrilled about his stature, I quietly wondered if the evident contentment had anything to do with being in the same small club as Keith.

Keith—older, confident, capable, quick of mind and quick of tongue—is a pretty cool kid. The more I thought about it, the more certain I was that my son will be in much better shape, long-term, if he takes his cues about size from Keith and not from me.

By this point I was absolutely lightheaded from all the anxiety. Finally exhaling, I tried to sound as normal as possible.

"True. You *are* small for your age."

I'd said it. It was out there. I tried not to sound too thrilled or too devastated as I spoke the words. Just a happy medium. Not even happy, really, just . . . purposefully average. I really think I did a pretty good job—for someone so thoroughly warped by this culture's craziness anyway.

It's funny how some of us just get so skittish about *admitting* that we notice things like size, color, gender, age, ethnic features and visibly recognizable disabilities—even though there's nothing particularly wrong about noticing differences. It's not like we're fooling anyone (besides ourselves, anyway). No woman who's eight feet tall, or one who's a little person, or one who uses a wheelchair, or one who's a supermodel, or one whose ethnic background is noticeably different from ours, or one who is morbidly obese, or one who lives with a facial disfigurement, or one who is ninety-seven years old: no woman who is any of these things honestly believes that you don't *notice*. She knows you do.

The problem isn't the noticing.

SQUEEZE

I became keenly aware of this not too long ago, as my twentieth high school reunion approached. I'd known it was coming for about, oh . . . twenty years. The tenth reunion went off all right, but I had higher hopes for twenty. Twice as high. Anyway, twelve months before it came due, I thought to myself, *If I could lose forty or fifty pounds this year, I would be looking fine at that reunion.* One year seemed like plenty of time to pull off such an amazing feat of nature.

Nine months before the reunion, I had done nothing toward the end of looking fantastic at my class gathering. *Nine months,* I reasoned: *that should still be enough time to make this thing happen. With the right diet and exercise I have got to be looking better than I do now. I can do this.*

Time passed. Six months before the reunion I was still scarfing down pizza and eating too many cheesy quesadillas. I exercised regularly, but not enough to offset all the yummy cheese.

Then, at the three-month marker, a single thought garnered my entire attention. You know who I started thinking about at the three-month marker? I began perseverating on Tom Hanks. I started thinking about how skinny he got playing a poor guy stranded on a desert island in that movie *Castaway.* I said to myself, *Movie stars like Tom Hanks have to lose lots of weight all the time. Then they put it all back on pretty quickly. And in the biz, time is money. So these stars probably have to lose thirty, forty or sixty pounds in three months. They probably do it all the time in the biz. And if Tom can do it, I can do it.* This is exactly what I said to myself. Then I ate a slice of pizza.

Before I knew it, the reunion was just one week away. As reality hit me like a cold splash in the face, I was no longer thinking about movie stars. I *was* still delusional, though. Prayerfully, standing before the bathroom mirror, I pointed to the ugly red blemish under my saggy chin and instructed, "God, if we could just do something about this blemish before the reunion, that would be great."

I am such a mess.

Who was I even trying to impress? There was no old flame. There was no new flame. There was no frowned-upon teacher crush. There was no sinister cheerleader archenemy. So who was I even trying to impress? I had no idea.

I hated that I cared about the eyes of others.

Ten People Whose Judgment About My Body Is Entirely Irrelevant

1. *People who will evaluate what I'm wearing in church*

2. *People who see me wearing unflattering Lycra while doing cardio*

3. *People who are younger than me*

4. *People who are older than me*

5. *People my age*

6. *The mail carrier*

7. *People leaner than me*

8. *People chunkier than me*

9. *Men*

10. *Women*

TRACY

A few summers ago, during our family's annual beach vacation, my in-laws took all their children and grandchildren to a matinee showing of *Hairspray*. The remake of the 1988 movie is based on the hit Broadway musical. The outing was a huge success, enjoyed by all. The feel-good musical left every last man, woman and child in the theater feeling not-so-horrible about going to a dark movie theater when we all should have been outside frolicking on the sunny beach.

The movie opens as an overweight teenager, Tracy Turnblad, dresses and makes her way to school. The delightful girl, endearing from the moment she graces the screen, shows no evidence of caring that she isn't considered one of the pretty, popular girls at school. That, in my book, is irresistible. Honestly, Tracy Turnblad makes fat look fantastic! I would not be one bit surprised to learn that skinny girls envied Tracy's contentment and sunny outlook on life. This does not happen in the movie, but I wouldn't be surprised to learn that it happened privately in dark movie theaters.

John Travolta plays Tracy's mother. Bearing inordinate shame about her weight, Edna Turnblad represents the antithesis of Tracy's own self-acceptance. Ashamed of being seen in public, she hasn't left her home in years. I suspect many of us can easily relate to the self-consciousness of Tracy's mother. Sure, we leave our homes, but while we're doing it, we *do* care what people think when they see us.

Over the course of the movie, though, Mrs. Edna Turnblad learns to ignore—yea, *shun*—the judging eyes of others. Finally able to embrace her full figure, she at last starts living.

The final dance scene is as inspiring as any Spirit-filled church service, although in a different way. Its clear message of salvation is proclaimed, on live television, to the entire metropolitan Baltimore area as Edna boldly proclaims,

So if you don't like the way I look, well I just don't give a d**n!
'Cause the world keeps spinning round and round,
And my heart's keeping time to the speed of sound,
I was lost 'til I heard the drums and I found my way.

I once was lost and now am found. This is what I'm saying about the inspirational nature of the film.

I want to be Edna Turnblad. Maybe not with the heart disease and knee problems, but I want to live into the freedom of not caring what other people think of me. I want to move through the world with a "So if you don't like the way I look, well, I just don't give a care" attitude.

I suspect Jesus might have. Without the cursing.

6

GLUTTONY

Enough *Really Is* Enough

While wrestling a shopping cart free in the grocery store foyer a few months ago, a bright neon poster caught my eye. The sign featured this critical alert: ALL YOUR HALLOWEEN NEEDS ON AISLE 12! There was a day when I might have made a beeline to aisle twelve. Smiling to myself that day, though, I wondered what the big *need* could possibly be. Fake cobwebs? Gummy eyeballs? Honestly, keeping myself from doctoring the misleading sign with the black Sharpie I had in my purse took more self-control than avoiding the holiday necessities. As a rule of thumb, whenever the word *need* is modified by a holiday whose distinguishing feature is candy, be prepared to ask some questions.

GIVE US THIS DAY . . .

"Give us this day our daily bread." Even though we say it—some of us every week—I can't help but wonder if we really mean it.

Though we say it with our mouths, too often our lives breathe a different message. Rather, the prayer we live hollers, "I've taken my daily bread, thank you. Actually, two portions of the stuff I like. And dessert. With vitamin water on the side. And some costly calorie-burning supplements. And the Ben & Jerry's I will have *earned* once I get home from the gym." That's what we do.

Don't even get me started on daily caffeinated beverages.

Most Americans consume not only *our* daily bread, but the daily portion meant for Lupita, Rani, Kyung Ja, Dahlia and Rasheta as well. The resources we continue to consume in food, drink, clothing and housing make a mockery of our prayer.

Father, forgive us, for we care not what we do.

Personally, I'm a big fan of the daily bread. I most enjoy mine flattened into a circle, slathered with tomato sauce and suffocated under way too much cheese. If I had to choose one type of *bread* to eat *daily* for the rest of my life, pizza would be it. What always trips me up is the portion size. This is because my personal preference is to enjoy two or three *daily* portions in one sitting. I am always baffled when I watch people who can eat one or two slices of pizza, wipe their greasy fingers on a napkin and stop eating. I so respect that kind of fortitude.

I wish I were that lean, sensible woman, but I'm just not.

Like so many women, I've had my struggles around food. Many of these involve pizza. Typically, I'll do one of two things on pizza night. I will either polish off half the pie, or I will eat none of it. Most often it's been the former. If I've abstained and it's late winter or springtime, I've most likely given up pizza or cheese for the season of Lent. If it's not Lent and I pass it by, then there's no question: I've given it up for the entire year. For years, those two tunes—gluttony and abstinence—were the only Oreo and pizza songs I knew. It's certainly more than a little embarrassing to admit that.

Sadly, this is how I've been. For most of my life I've been an "all or nothing" girl. During my fifteenth year, away at summer camp, I survived on water, lettuce and bran cereal for five weeks. I highly discourage that monotonous diet. Then, for a few years in my early twenties, it seemed like I was always swearing off something. If it wasn't pizza for Lent, it was a year without desserts. Along the way, more reasonable friends—which included just about everyone I knew—encouraged me to give moderation a shot.

"Why not just eat one or two pieces of pizza?" they'd ask gently.

"Yeah, that would be great, it really would," I'd agree. "I've just never really been able to pull it off." It's hard to argue with decades of failure.

I could heartily agree that eating normal healthy portions was the superior way, but in my weakness I just couldn't do it. I hadn't given up the hope of sensible consumption, and I truly hoped that someday I would become that person. Until then, however, I'd have to keep swearing off stuff.

What always complicates sinful matters is that when others would notice me declining yummy Crisco-frosted Costco birthday cake or gently refusing a warm gooey brownie, they'd celebrate my moral fortitude. *I* knew, though. I knew that my anxious death-grip about staying in control was as death-dealing as overindulgence might have been.

In recent months I've actually come closer than I've ever been before to practicing moderation. For me, it's one of those important growing edges as I follow Jesus. I'm just not entirely comfortable acting like I've got it all figured out yet.

NEEDS AND WANTS

Part of our trouble distinguishing *want* from *need* has been complicated by a fuzzy vocabulary situation. For years I threw around the word *need* when it really wasn't the most accurate choice of words. "I need a Diet Coke." "I need mascara." "I need shoes." "I need socks." What might have been more accurate would have been to exchange the word *need* for the word *want*.

If I had been more honest with myself, I would have admitted, *The Diet Coke I want right now would be so pleasing and tasty.*

I would have realized, *I want a second tube of mascara to keep in my backpack because—since I don't even think to use the stuff most of the time—I can never find it. When I eventually do experience an eyelash emergency, perhaps while backpacking through the Alps, having an extra tube will increase my odds of actually having some on hand. Because who knows when calamity will strike? Quite possibly in the Alps. That's why I want to buy mascara.*

If I had been completely honest, I would have admitted, *I want new shoes. Specifically, I want shoes that will match one or two of my favorite cutie outfits that I love to wear. Or maybe my next book cover.*

When I was browsing online at Sock Dreams, I could have confessed, *I don't actually need socks. Between my husband and my big-footed self, we probably have at least four dozen pairs of adult socks in our home—which means that, at this point, I already would only have to do sock laundry every three or four weeks. Though I have some boring solid-color socks to match a few of my outfits, I sure don't own any of these groovy green- and orange-striped socks I'm seeing online that come all the way up over the knee on normal-sized people. Nor do I own a pair of black socks with white polka dots that now beckon to me like some textile harlot. I want some polka-dot socks.*

This whole vocabulary situation is critical, people, for those of us who really want to be truthtellers. Let's all say *want* when we mean *want*, so that we can save *need* for much more important matters. These might include life-saving drugs for those who've just survived Hurricane Katrina, water for the dehydrated in Phoenix, raincoats for teens who live on the streets in Seattle and down jackets for the underclothed who live in icy cold Buffalo, New York. Not polka-dot socks.

HARDNESS OF HEART

For too many years I bought the quiet lie that the socks or the beverage or the shoes would actually satisfy. My better judgment clouded by the thrill of each purchase, I'd drive home happily with my crinkly white plastic shopping bags sitting on the passenger seat beside me.

Three blocks from home, I would drive past drug deals going down on the street or sidewalk next to my car. Glancing out the window at the precious, desperate customers, I'd note to myself how sad it was that, once that hit wore off, mothers and fathers and sons and daughters would soon be back for another. Solemnly, spiritually, I would grieve the broken relationships and misspent resources that each illicit purchase represented. Then I'd start thinking about where I might have left the scissors so I could start cutting price tags off the jackets and jeans and jerseys I had bought the second I got home.

Sadly, I failed to recognize the disturbing similarities between myself and my differently hungry neighbors. I now suspect this was due to the sort of heart-hardening requisite to justify whatever unnecessary purchases I had just made. The price of that chosen dullness—the quenching of the Spirit's gentle insistence—was more costly than the clothes.

And yet, despite the wily nature of sin, the Spirit, who is gracious and ever-resourceful, continues to lead, teach and shepherd. As we finally concede to cooperate, by resisting the temptation to satisfy every impulse, the integrity of our relationships with God and with others are nourished and strengthened. As we learn to say "enough is enough" and live it, we're freed up from the gluttonous consumption that has been hardening our hearts to noticing and responding to the legitimate needs of others.

Our culture has conditioned us to please ourselves by consuming as much as we can, for as little as we can, as often as we can. Being completely satisfied once our needs have been met, even daring to resist a want or two, can be a bit confounding to Americans. What's most disturbing is that it even baffles the Christians who ask God to meet our needs every week.

7

OBJECTIFICATION

How Women Agree
with Our Thingification

Pawing through the racks at Kmart, looking for a shirt for my daughter, I felt disappointed by the lame selection. Most of the toddler-size shirts were printed with unsatisfying messages like "Spoiled Rotten" and "Sexy Beast." Continuing to dig, I finally found one I could handle. It read simply, "Dancer." The illustration featured a girl with a huge head and a tiny body who was, in fact, dancing. I just knew that my daughter would love the white shirt with turquoise sleeves and lots of glitter. Truly, with all the glitter, it could have read "Yucky" and she would have loved it.

On the way to preschool the next morning, I glanced back in the rearview mirror to admire my sparkly girl. What I saw just about stopped my heart. Though she was buckled into her big-girl booster seat, head bent down, Zoë was carefully rolling up her shirt in order to bare her sweet, roundish, toddler midriff.

I squinted to see whatever it was that Zoë was looking at that had inspired her to show some skin. To my horror, it was Dancer Girl. Apparently I'd failed to inspect what Dancer was wearing on her miniature little body. That's right: the big-headed dancer was wearing a shirt that exposed tiny cartoon abs.

It was hard to know whether to laugh or cry. In three short years my daughter had learned—from T-shirts and from magazines and from noticing girls at church and from the nearby mall where we went only for free carousel rides—that there was power in exposing more of her body than was really necessary.

Three years old.

As it began to sink in, crying suddenly seemed a much more appropriate response than laughing.

SQUEEZED

My daughter understood, intuitively, that our culture *does* value those who, with their physical bodies, attract positive attention. Every day girls and women are bombarded with images on our televisions, computers, phones and mailboxes that remind us of the culture's clear priorities.

The problem for women and girls who call ourselves followers of Jesus is that the culture's values ultimately collide with the ones we claim to hold. A lot of us claim to be patterning our lives after Jesus—the guy who is undeniably self-sacrificing, other-referenced and downwardly mobile—but in our heart of hearts, given our druthers, we'd really prefer to look *hot* while we do it. With the choices we make and the dollars we spend, we endorse the culture's madness by agreeing that our bodies exist to be viewed.

We were made for so much more.

I want to imagine, for you and for me, what *more* looks like. As we look toward the person of Jesus, as we notice the ways that God moves in human flesh, we begin to see it. As we notice the physical rhythms of the body of Jesus—kneeling for prayer, rising toward friendship, extending his hand to the hungry, touching the sick—we begin to glimpse the thing for which these bodies were made. As we listen to the witness of Scripture and eyeball the person of Jesus, we notice a body that is not an object in itself, but one that moves toward others in love. We see a body which is made, not to be viewed, but for relationship. Just like ours.

THINGIFICATION

When we value girls and women for how their bodies appear, we do something that theologian Paul Tillich and Martin Luther King Jr. called "thingification." It means exactly what you think it might. When a girl or woman is valued for her appearance, she has been thingified. When a woman's image appears on a pornographic website, she has been thingified. When a seventeen-year-old sends out a revealing photo of herself snapped on her cell phone, she has thingified herself. When, on the cover of a popular women's magazine, a famous actress's body parts have been digitally enlarged, reduced, colored, fluffed and reshaped—even though we all thought she was beautiful in the first place—she has been thingified. The added heartbreak, in this modern strain of objectification, is that the possibility of any kind of organized resistance occurs to so few of us. Instead, most of us participate willingly.

We actually embrace this ungodly situation as if it were a great idea. When a physically attractive young woman in college makes extra money by working as an "exotic dancer," she *cooperates* with her thingification. When we as women, both young and old, systematically alter every body part imaginable with cosmetics and dyes and elective surgery, we *agree* to our thingification. When mothers insist that daughters dress in clothes and shoes that restrict their movement in order to appear attractive to others, at age four or fourteen or twenty-four, we *participate* in their thingification.

Come on, Margot, you might be thinking. *You did not just put exotic dancing in the same category as eye shadow. I really wanted to agree with you, but now you've lost all credibility. You should have just stayed with the sexually revealing stuff so that all of us who would never have a* chance *of being hired as strippers could all be a little outraged with you at women who participate in their own thingification. You really had me until the mascara.*

I get this, I really do. I have had exactly the same reaction to that whacky apostle Paul, who made these long lists of practices to avoid and chose to stick *envy* right next to *murder*. What kind of a weird dirty trick is that anyway? So I completely understand that all my friends who are makeup-wearers and hair-dyers might be feeling more than a little bent out of shape, now that I've included them in the ranks of pole strippers.

Author and truth-teller extraordinaire Anne Lamott gets this. She recognizes how easily we cooperate with our thingification. For example, in *Grace Eventually*, Lamott says,

> This culture's pursuit of beauty is a crazy, sick, losing game, for women, men, teenagers, and with the need to increase advertising revenues, now for pre-adolescents, too. . . . Every time we agree to play another round, and step out onto the court to try again, we've already lost. The only way to win is to stay off the court.

I'm aware that my size-twelve feet have just stepped on some well-manicured toes, but it had to be said. Stay off the court, sisters. And keep your cut abs, and your flabby ones, to yourself.

8

SELF-PREOCCUPATION

The Boiling Frog Syndrome

I had just driven four hours, to the mountains, in order to spend the weekend with a women's group. I knew that these women were from a new church start-up, but when I arrived I didn't yet know anyone personally.

For reasons that are much too elaborate to explain here, I'd made the trip to the mountains in a roomy black Lycra outfit, on top and bottom. The entire ride I'd been feeling cozy and comfortable and maybe just a little bit proud that I had been so smart to accidentally travel in such comfortable clothes. Somewhere along my westward route, I'd even made a mental note to wear that exact stretchy outfit the next time I flew across the country. I was also wearing my jazzy orange denim jacket, so the ensemble wasn't quite as boring as it might have sounded at first.

Parking my car in a gravel lot, I dragged some of my stuff into the lodge where we would all be staying. On the way in, I met a clump of the young women who'd arrived a few hours earlier. Most of them were in their twenties. Dressed in jeans and T-shirts, they were on their way out to grab an early dinner and invited me to come along.

Rather than concentrating on learning some new names and faces, this is what I was thinking as I was meeting them: *Too much Lycra. I am wearing too much Lycra and looking like a middle-aged woman who doesn't fit into her skinny jeans anymore.* I really felt panicked. *Why will these young, cool hipsters care about a single word I have to say this weekend? How could I have done this? What was I thinking by showing up in Lycra? I hope I haven't blown the whole weekend with this. Honestly, I wouldn't blame them for writing me off.* In my mind, the entire credibility of the gospel had been jeopardized by the Lycra.

"Yeah, I'd love to grab some dinner," I said too loudly, to distract attention from my stretchy pants. "I'm just gonna drop this stuff in my room." *And change my clothes like lightning,* I thought to just myself. In nanoseconds I was wearing jeans, a green stripy shirt and a sweatshirt. And it's not like I was posing, I tried to convince myself. I did *pack* that cute outfit. I really do like to be as casual as the next girl. Feeling more comfortable—though that really shouldn't have been possible, given all the Lycra—I rejoined the group.

After enjoying a tasty dinner, I headed back to my room to get ready. The evening program was scheduled to begin at seven. I probably should have been more prayerful during that window of time, but I had accessories to deal with. I was wearing my favorite lime green glasses and some new green earrings I'd picked up on the way to the mountains. So I'd match. I had no idea where my cutie green rhinestone nose ring was so, with a little disappointment, I had to let that go. I tossed a green necklace I'd recently made around my neck. I'd found those fantastic beads, with a white spiral swirl in the middle of each one, at a bead store near my mom's home in California. I pulled on a pair of my favorite socks, blue and green, and then slid my feet into shoes I'd recently gotten for my birthday. Eco-friendly, they were lime green slides and . . . wait for it . . . they had a single white swirl—*like the necklace*—on the side of each one. Fantastic, right? I know. Wearing blue jeans and the same shirt I'd worn an hour earlier at dinner, I convinced myself that I was just like everyone else who had casually thrown on jeans and a tee to do some straight-up chillin' in the mountains.

Grabbing my book bag, I wandered down to the auditorium where the meetings would be held. Most of the women had not yet arrived. The music team and planning team were preparing for the program.

"Those are *awesome* glasses," one woman marveled. "They go great with your necklace."

"Thanks," I smiled. "I like them too."

I slipped out to use the restroom, where I bumped into another woman on the retreat.

"Oh my gosh! Those shoes are fabulous! Where did you get them?!" she raved.

"Well," I began humbly, "my mother-in-law wanted to get me shoes for my birthday and I just kind of found them . . ." I tried to use a calm voice that would give no indication of how screamy thrilled I was when I actually did come across those great shoes.

After I'd done my business, I was washing my hands.

"I love your necklace!" said another stranger. That's when it hit me.

I looked way too fabulous.

I really did. In that horribly complimentary moment, I experienced the stab of painful anguish that Peter must have endured after denying Jesus three times. Having sworn he would never do it, Peter had never even seen it coming. Neither had I. When the cock crowed about how fantastic my green necklace was, though, like Peter, I saw my sin flash before my eyes.

How on earth had it happened?

I mentally reviewed the evening. In the prayerful moments I had finally found, once I was completely accessorized, I had asked the Spirit to guide me as I stood onstage to tell these precious women that appearances don't matter all that much. The thing that really *does* matter, I would assure them, is being *for* others, the way that Jesus had been *for* us. Somehow, though, I had ended up looking so incredible that I wouldn't even blame them if they thought I was full of baloney. If I saw me, I'd probably think I was full of baloney, too.

Thankfully, in addition to helping public speakers articulate things meaningfully, the Spirit has other irons in the fire—like convicting hearts.

It is hard to know where to begin thinking about what went wrong that night. Without even realizing it—like a really cute green frog in a slowly boiling pot of water—I'd been gradually squeezed by the culture's pressure to look casually fantastic.

A study out of Duke University coined a term for this very thing—the appearance of looking way too fabulous, and yet as if one hadn't tried very hard at all. The study calls it "effortless perfection." It's a lie, of course—both the effortless and the perfection—but I'd played right into it. What was inherently *wrong* is that, for most of the evening, my eyes had been turned upon myself.

That's what went most wrong.

What is particularly sinister about our culture's fixation with beauty, and with my personal one, is that it keeps our eyes turned upon ourselves. As a reminder to avoid that wily temptation, I vowed that night, to just myself, that I would purposely never look so fantastic again.

And I do not believe I have.

Hear me: I don't have a beef with people appearing attractive. Please feel free to look entirely gorgeous around me. I simply mention it to note that since that evening I've been freed up, to a degree, from trying to look casually impeccable. I still enjoy coordinating my colors, but the pressure's off to have the watchband match the stitching on the sock toe that accentuates the fourth freckle from the nose ring. In fact, in the noble tradition of skilled

Amish quilters—who intentionally drop a stitch in order to honor their conviction that God alone is perfect—I will occasionally forgo the ring that matches the earrings or the hairclips that match the glasses. On purpose. To appear not *quite* so effortlessly perfect.

The irony is not lost on me that it requires a measure of additional, concerted effort to *not* appear as if I'm *not* trying, but I think it's worth it.

SELF

Many of us think about ourselves, and our bodies, *all day long*.

"Yeah," you might agree, "but how do you *not* do that?" That's the real question.

Telling someone not to think about themselves is like telling someone not to think about a pink elephant. Only, instead of an elephant, it's more like telling them to not to think . . . thoughts. Deciding not to think about ourselves, not to dwell on our bodies, is no small feat.

If we are to succeed, we sort of need a better plan.

Pastor and author Tim Keller mentions, in one of his sermons, the way that C. S. Lewis describes this humble sort of person who's not so obsessed with himself. "Do not imagine," writes Lewis, "that if you meet a really humble man he will be what most people call 'humble' nowadays: he will not be a sort of greasy, smarmy person, who is always telling you that, of course, he is nobody."

Please stay focused and try not to be distracted trying to visualize a greasy, smarmy person.

Lewis continues, "Probably all you will think about him is that he seemed a cheerful, intelligent chap who took a real interest in what you said to him."[1] If you've ever encountered someone like that, someone who is genuinely interested in what you're saying,

---

[1] C. S. Lewis, *Mere Christianity* (San Francisco: HarperSanFrancisco), p. 128.

you know how fantastic it is to be in their presence.

Did you catch that movement? Our eyes are freed up from being glued to ourselves when they are turned toward others. Granted, this is sort of a chicken-and-egg situation. Which comes first? Do we have to be freed from self-obsession first, before we can turn completely toward another? That seems like a tall, unlikely order. Or could it be that when we purpose to be concerned about someone else, when we take little dropped-stitch baby steps to make it happen, that's when the magic happens and we're liberated from having to think about ourselves so much.

I see an awful lot of hope in the latter. For everyone. However it happens, the shift from obsessive introspection to other-centered living is the movement into which we're called.

EXO-SPECTION

Sometimes the magic happens when we least expect it. I used to love to go out dancing with friends, wearing my favorite funky clothes. Recently, I got sort of dolled-up for a night out on the town with a few women friends. Our night out, of course, meant ordering takeout and sitting on my friend's porch until it got too buggy. But I'd been looking forward to it because I couldn't even remember the last time I'd gone out—or *in*, for that matter—with my women friends to a place that did not involve sand or slides.

I had gotten ready, as I so often do, in a bit of a rush. I should say I'm not a rusher by nature. Because I don't give my appearance lots and lots of attention on normal days, though, I just forget to add in extra time, to the usual *no* time, when the special days roll around. This was the precise situation in which I found myself. I barely made it into clothes before racing out the door. Truthfully, I was pretty thrilled to have gotten a shower.

My last responsibility, before a fun evening of having none, was to pick up my neighbor and drop her off at her dance class. Although I was a wee bit disappointed that no one at her dance class asked where I might be going looking so fantastic, after dropping off my friend I felt relieved to finally be on my way. Glancing down, I admired my daisy-painted boots, black- and white-striped knee socks, and black dress with tiny white polka dots.

My joy over my garments evaporated the moment I peeked in the rearview mirror. What was looking back at me was pretty visually disappointing.

It wasn't a makeup situation. I was okay with the accidental fact that I hadn't worn makeup. I had considered it, but then had gotten caught up wrapping a present for the friend whose birthday we'd be celebrating. I was even okay with the fact that, on my way to grab earrings, I'd somehow gotten detoured in order to help my son find his baseball uniform. So, no earrings. Resigned to the fact that I wouldn't be wearing a necklace or any of my favorite rings, I had run into the kitchen at the last possible second, turned off the oven and scribbled a sign for the counter: DINNER IN OVEN. Grabbing the birthday gift I had shoved into a red and green gift bag that read *Season's Greetings* (in May), I had raced out to the car, not wanting to be late to pick up my neighbor.

When I glanced in the mirror, though, what I saw looking back at me were blue glasses. That's right: *blue*. The ones I'd meant to wear, the black ones with little white polka dots, were still at home. Like I said: disappointing.

Blue glasses?! I was really off my game. How on earth had that happened?

As soon as the question drifted into my mind, the answer did too. I knew exactly what had happened since the last carefree time I'd gotten all gussied up to go out on the town with friends. I had married and become a mother to humans who eat dinner and play baseball. I had made a new friend, whose birthday I was so happy to be celebrating. I had offered a ride to a transportation-challenged neighbor who is a joyful dancer.

Suddenly, blue glasses didn't seem quite so bad.

I'm not saying I've become that humble, exo-spective person C. S. Lewis was describing. Certainly not on purpose. I do think, though, that as we're drawn outside of ourselves, freed up from thinking about ourselves so stinkin' much—even by accident— we find ourselves on the right track.

GOSPEL SELF-ESTEEM

My friend Travis gets this. He's on staff at Remuda Ranch, a center specializing in the treatment of those living with eating disorders. Travis is also a cofounder of the True Campaign, which sponsors a program called "true:shift." The program gives women the opportunity to partner with Food for the Hungry, through which they get to tangibly participate in this liberating shift toward others in need. In the process, they become free from a crippling preoccupation with themselves. See how that's kind of a naturally fabulous two-fer?

Travis recently blogged about a new study claiming that college girls suffering from eating disorders who became involved in compassionate, "other-centered" activities saw a decrease in the symptoms. Pretty cool, huh? Travis continues, "I'm not suggesting a degrading of oneself or promoting passivity. In fact, what I like to call 'gospel self-esteem' is far more powerful than simply trying to convince yourself that you are valuable through positive self-talk and affirmations. Based on an understanding that we have incredible value as creations of God and that he is committed to our good without ignoring our failure, gospel self-esteem means trusting that what God says about me is true. That is the basis for incredible boldness and liberating humility."

Travis continues on to share what that dynamite Tim Keller calls "blessed self-forgetfulness": "a healthy self-image where you are not thinking more of yourself or thinking less of yourself in false humility, but thinking of yourself less."

And how yummy is that?! Don't you just wanna run out and get a great big piece o' that good stuff?

9
FREEDOM

Chain Saw Liberation

We're ready to live differently.

Unfortunately, the church has not yet succeeded in drawing women into a compelling expression of bodily discipleship. Though we've been assured that God finds us *beautiful*—maybe in our hearts, or in some divine otherworldly dimension or possibly with divine x-ray goggles—this well-meant reassurance has not yet set us free. Don't get me wrong: I would *like* to embrace that wonderful concept. I really would. It's just that—I'm familiar with my heart. Not all of it is pretty. God knows I'm a garden-variety sinner like the rest of humanity. I've never once heard God whispering in my ear that I'm gorgeous and fantastically perfect on the inside. I'm just not.

Outside either, for that matter.

Some of us have been assured that God made us *exactly as we are*, so we darn well better be pleased with the body God chose for us. As much as I love that idea, and as much as I'd like to blame God for some of the extra rolls around my middle, I can't honestly say that the Almighty is the one who's been eating too much pizza. Neither can I stomach the corollary that God is purposefully assigning disability and debilitating disease and death. Rather, that seems to be the stuff from which God, in Jesus Christ, is *delivering* those of us who dwell in mortal bodies, both now and in the coming kingdom.

Though Christian women today *long* to believe the inspiring religious assurances that God thinks we're spiritual knockouts, in our bones, most of us do not. I am of the mind that this is the better part of wisdom. After all, should we really be expected to believe that God is looking over plump affluent women, and bone-thin starving ones, spending as much time and energy finding us all beautiful as we spend *wishing* that we were? That's pretty hard to swallow, what with all the affluence and hunger going on.

I'm not even convinced that our beauty matters to God quite as much as we think it does. It seems like *we're* the ones who get all jazzed about the importance of our own appearances, whether outer or inner. Then most of us just end up stuck, jammed somewhere between the culture's unattainable standard of outer beauty—which is so very *easy* to buy into—and the pat assurance that God thinks we're knockouts on the inside—which, if we're honest, is actually much harder to believe. I'm just afraid that when we put all our eggs in the beauty basket, even the spiritual eggs, we miss the big point of what God has in mind for these bodies. God just seems to be dealing in an entirely different currency than we've been working with, until now, when it comes to the value and purpose of our bodies.

Women of faith are itchy to live differently. Some of us have already had an inkling that there is more to life than unnaturally perky breasts and tightly sculpted abs. We've begun to suspect that these bodies have a higher purpose than looking fantastic—to God's glory, of course—in Sunday morning worship. Squinting, noticing other women who seem comfortable in their own skins, we've begun to catch glimpses of an intriguing new kingdom way. After all, we're the ones who declare that we've been entirely *accepted* by God through Jesus Christ. And yet so many of us continue to limp along as if we're not really acceptable. Surely, we reason, Jesus' redemption can't possibly extend to these thighs.

Can't it?

It's got to.

In my prayerful imagination, I see Jesus standing right in the center of the tug-of-war between the culture's unachievable standard of beauty and the hard-to-grasp truth about God's admiration of our pure hearts. Jesus is holding a huge chain saw. Then, lifting that massive instrument, he buzzes right through the chaos and leaves that strangling, death-dealing rope in two pieces on the ground, like a dead cobra. Then he motions us with his finger to come along and discover the better way that's found in him.

In describing this sort of situation to his first followers, Jesus cautioned folks to be on guard when a demon—maybe like the nasty one named "our culture's insane enslavement to physical beauty"—was expelled from them. When that demon couldn't find a new home in which to live, Jesus warned, the demon would come back, find the place empty and take up residence again, inviting seven family members to move in with him.

It's a little like that when we decide we're not going to be bossed around by the world's values anymore. If no *new* life is generated in us where the old has been expelled, there's no reason we *won't* be sucked in once again to the world's warped whirlpool of values. If we've decided *not* to be about a dreadful preoccupation with ourselves, then we need to be about something else.

What we quickly discover about the new Jesus way is that mental assent is not enough. This new way must be *walked*, must be *embodied*. It must be *lived*. Embracing this different way means that we will begin to make new choices and establish new practices. One place to start might be to sculpt a sexy mannequin piñata—with pages from all the magazines featuring the gorgeous Photoshopped women who don't really exist—and smash it to pieces. Perhaps it will catch on as a cutting-edge twenty-first-century spiritual discipline.

As we begin to live differently, and move our bodies differently, we're liberated from the suffocating corset that we hadn't even realized had been choking the Spirit's breath right out of us. As our Maker breathes new life into these nostrils, lips and bones—and as we're fueled by that breath—we are finally set free to do the thing for which we were made: love others with our hearts, souls, minds and strength.

We already knew what our bodies weren't for. Now we're choosing to embrace and celebrate what they are for.

10

VALUE

Living into a New Reality

Whenit comes to mass-emailed stories, jokes, photos and video links, I have a relatively firm "don't read and quickly delete" policy.

My friend MJ got me today, though, by starting her email, "You probably all know what I'm talking about if you've seen the news today." I didn't and I hadn't. I certainly didn't want to be the only person who didn't know and hadn't seen. So, against my better judgment, I clicked.

It was a clip from one of those talent search shows called *Britain's Got Talent*. That cynical Simon Cowell was one of the judges. The clip begins by introducing us to a contestant named Susan Boyle. Everything about Susan Boyle is—by Hollywood's standard of beauty—wrong. Sure, we'll tolerate physical imperfection for the first few episodes of *The Biggest Loser*, but typically we don't have a lot of patience for much besides the kind of glam we've been conditioned to expect. And deserve.

Ms. Boyle introduces herself to the camera, "My name is Susan Boyle. I'm nearly forty-eight, currently unemployed but still looking, and I'm going to sing for you on *Britain's Got Talent* today." She continues, "At the moment I live alone with my cat called Pebbles. I've never been married. I've never been kissed." Then, flashing a look of mock sadness, she playfully bemoans, "Oh, shame!" At the end of the clip, squinting her eyes in determination, Susan Boyle promises with steely resolve, "I'm going to make that audience *rock*." I assume she most likely said more stuff, but producers cropped it just to highlight the particularly uncomfortable and socially awkward parts. The subtext of the editing, of course, is to lure us all into agreeing that Susan Boyle isn't worth very much by the world's standards. Judging from the audience's facial expressions, it worked. As the soundtrack from *Les Mis* begins, though, Susan Boyle has only to pipe out eight words before minds and faces are radically changed. "I dreamed a dream in time gone by . . ." By the time she gets to "by," she has been justified. Well-manicured judging eyebrows rise. Eyes widen. Audience members begin clapping, whistling. Before long the audience has risen to their feet, wild with adulation.

I'm not particularly musical, but even I knew that I was listening to, and watching, a truly gifted woman.

We love this stuff, don't we? We eat it up. It's even *better* than a Cinderella story, because this Cinderella is too old, too heavy, too gray, too unsophisticated. In a word, she's *us*. Except with talent.

And that's the single piece of this great story that leaves me unsettled. We all feel warm and fuzzy inside, whether we're seated in the actual television audience or watching the clip on YouTube. Some part of us feels generous for applauding someone who doesn't fit into the world's mold of acceptability. So bravo for us for being so open-minded.

In the end, though, Susan Boyle still had to *earn* the approval and praise of her audience. She had to *prove* that she was worthy of acceptance. Sure, it's sort of the nature of a talent competition, but if we're really honest, it's sort of the nature of the world, too.

In my fantasies, I like to imagine a world where Susan Boyle swaggers out on stage and gets the standing ovation for no other reason than that she reflects the image of God. Wouldn't that be the most fabulous place?

GOD'S REALITY

I happen to live exactly .96 miles from such an alternate cosmos. On Tuesday nights I get to hang out there, at the Reality Center, with my teenage friends with and without disabilities. The Tuesday Night Live experience is one part of an organization called Reality Ministries.

As we're eating our pizza, every person is invited to jot down some bit of news from the week. Then as the meal winds down and we're nibbling away at our Chips Ahoy cookies, a few microphoned news anchors—typically grinning, young college or high school women—will read "Friendz Newz" out loud for the rest of us to hear.

"And now for Friendz Newz!" one announces. "Carolyn will be traveling to Germany over the summer." Everyone claps and cheers for Carolyn. A neighboring pizza-eater gives her a high five.

"This weekend Tyrone will be cheering for UNC." At this, half the room claps and cheers and the other half, loyal to the Duke Blue Devils, shouts the most joyful and delighted "boos" imaginable.

"Janine's birthday," the announcer begins, beaming, "is in one hundred and fifty-eight days!" As Janine stands to be recognized, the room bursts into applause.

One of the announcers asks the crowd for a drumroll. Jamel, who is never without his drumsticks, bangs the chair in front of him. The rest of us start slapping our thighs and tables and chairs in growing anticipation.

"Christopher," the announcer shouts, like maybe Christopher has won the lottery and is only finding out about it just now, "had CEREAL for BREAKFAST!!!!" At this, the room absolutely explodes in riotous cheering and applause. Raising one arm, cupping his hand in a royal wave, Christopher humbly acknowledges the crowd as if he might be the president of the United States, on inauguration day, riding in a heavily guarded entourage down Pennsylvania Avenue.

This sort of thunderous celebration continues on as we learn that Vicky had choir practice on Thursday, that Marcelle's brother is visiting and that Tanya will shop for new socks on Saturday.

Doesn't this sound like the most fabulous place in the world to be? Believe me, it is.

Sure, we all still feel warm and fuzzy inside, like everyone did cheering for Susan Boyle. What makes Reality Ministries so much more fantastic than the stage of a reality TV talent show, however, is that we've all agreed that every individual in the room is entirely acceptable and lovable and worthy for just . . . existing.

WHAT BODIES ARE FOR

With the announcements at Reality Ministries being so fantastic, you can only imagine what the annual talent show is like. It happened a few weeks ago.

I'd been traveling and was scheduled to arrive home moments before the show was scheduled to begin. Exhausted emotionally and physically the morning of the talent show I silently hoped to get snowed-in in Chicago on my way back from L.A. I truly am so selfish that I would secretly wish to take down an entire flight of other passengers to manage my guilt-free plan to get out of going to the talent show.

On any other night, this sort of celebration of my friends' gifts would absolutely pop my corn. Still crabbing about it as I left the house—having arrived home with ten minutes to spare—I picked up my friend Jackie who lives in a group home on my block. She was planning to dance in the show. I knew my friend DeCarlo was going to sing. Rodney, one of my favorite performers in the whole galaxy, would play his guitar. Me? I'm a closet introvert, so

I just planned to clap and smile and come home more emotionally exhausted than when I left.

My plan for the evening, however, was superseded by Someone Else's plan.

First the emcee, Cameron, came strutting out, spewing a thick Jersey accent and wearing a green blazer, white pants and a curly wig. Really, how can you go wrong with that getup? This began to cheer me up. He would introduce each act and then two lovely assistants, precious high school girls, would escort the delirious performers off the stage, just like at the Oscars.

Friends Hassan and Charlie danced their socks off. On a typical day, all you have to do is sneeze and Charlie will start dancing. It doesn't take much. Give him some actual music, and an audience, and he'll give you a performance that is off the hook.

Three high school girls, dressed in fancy matching cheerleading uniforms, led a cheer. Janine, the squad leader, who depends on a walker for mobility, got more height on her jumps than I do on mine. It was terribly impressive.

After the cheering, Leonard sang one of John Travolta's solos from the movie *Grease*. Clutching his chest at the sad parts, waving his arms and even dropping to his knees, Leonard's performance truly was Oscar-worthy.

Then Evan and Dave did a little freestyle hip-hop number. The crowd went wild, many jumping to their feet and dancing themselves. Now there's something you can't do at some fancy-schmancy opera or ballet performance. Not for long, anyway.

Allan read a poem in Hawaiian and then in English. I would have been impressed with just one of those languages.

When DeCarlo climbed onto the stage and grabbed a microphone, he *owned* that room. As the opening notes of gospel music began playing, he welcomed everyone. "Good evening!" he bellowed with the sort of commanding presence he might have developed if he'd spent twenty or thirty years pastoring a church in Vegas. Or playing the strip. "Y'all having a good time tonight?!

Praise the Lord!" It was as if he'd been born for that moment. While he was singing, our precious friend Patricia couldn't help herself and jumped onto the stage, too. For a moment, I toyed with the idea of dragging Patricia back down to ground level. I waited a moment, though, to see how others, and DeCarlo, would react. Every other person in the room besides uptight me was just thrilled that, like Fergie and JT and Lady Gaga, DeCarlo had a backup dancer.

Patricia stayed.

After DeCarlo and Patricia's number, Tommy climbed up on the stage and, taking the mike and facing the audience, described a large pastel drawing he'd created. It was a picture of Jesus in front of a brilliant blue sky with a fiery yellow sun. The words that Tommy had written at the bottom of the work read:

Paying Attention to God
Open Mind Open Heart
Voices of Silence
God is full of Passion for You
Jesus Christ, healer Savior Lord

Hanson demonstrated his mad skills as a DJ. Mona read a poem she'd chosen. Joel invited guests up for his uncanny imitation of *Who Wants to Be a Millionaire*. Rodney sang an amazing song he'd composed called "Celtic Woman." Jerry, who lives with autism, performed a beautifully fluent medley of songs. Linda read a Scripture passage she had read at her brother's wedding. Stan shared a poem he'd written.

No one that night *had* to be as fantastic as Susan Boyle, because everyone had caught on so quickly that every individual, on stage and off, was entirely acceptable and lovable and worthy for just . . . existing.

11

RECOGNIZABILITY

Water Park Epiphany

How many women, possibly a little disappointed with what they see in the mirror every morning, have wanted, on one day or another, to look like someone else? Though I don't have any hard statistical data on this, I'm going to guess and say *a bunch*. A great big bunch.

I am delighted to report that I am no longer among these.

I don't mean to sound braggy. It's just that, after years of being in that dissatisfied crowd, I finally saw the light last summer at Wet'n Wild Emerald Pointe water park in Greensboro, North Carolina. I realize not everyone experiences life-changing epiphanies while standing half-naked behind hundreds of other slippery people at a water park.

I, though, apparently do.

RIVER RAPIDS

I was standing in line for the Raging Rapids next to my nine-year-old daughter, Zoë. As we waited, I couldn't help but notice all the different bodies of the people who were pressed around us. No place else, save a sunny Saturday at the beach, can one witness so much surface area on so many different sizes and shapes and colors of bodies. At the beach, though, I would have been able to keep a much more comfortable distance.

To pass the time, I perused the vast assortment of bathing suits being worn that day, making a mental bar graph of the suit ratio between flowers and solids and stripes and polka dots and patterns. Underneath all the decorative suits, though, I started to notice the rich visual variety among the actual short and tall and medium bodies. Of course there was the predictable yummy palette of skin colors in hues of cocoa and peach and chocolate and cream. There was an endless variety of hair colors, too, in limp, wet and flattened styles. There were a few beards and locks, some braids, some tattoos. Some of the people around me, at first glance, looked mostly physically able, and others appeared to live with more physical challenges. I even glanced quickly, furtively, at stomachs and buttocks and hips and thighs. Some of them were full and squishy, the type with which I'm most familiar, while others were taut and lean. For that wonderfully rare, judgment-free moment—I'm not even sure how *that* happened—I just observed how different every *body* was.

Marveling at the sheer variety of human packaging, I found myself speculating about who might be *inside* each one. Even though I was only privy to the outside wrapper—to stuff like perky ponytails and angry eyebrows and flirty grins—I became aware that each different package hosted a distinct personality, a unique person, inside. Let the record show: I do not buy into any sort of weird bifurcation between *body* and *person*. I'm just reporting, here, the details of the water park epiphany. The unique design suggests that each intricately made person, worth knowing and distinguishing from all the other people on earth, had been marked by her Creator as recognizable by her unique physical features.

Isn't that sort of mind-boggling?

Though I've never had a sudden drug-induced heightened awareness, I think that if I had, it would have been something like what happened to me at the water park.

For years I had watched these horrible makeover shows that make women look like people they're not, all under the clever guise of boosting their attractiveness. In that instant, though, I finally understood why each face and each body had been created differently in the first place. I understood, intuitively, why God didn't decide to give each one of us identical matching trouble-free hair, cute perky noses, wide sparkly doe eyes, cut abs and cellulite-free thighs.

It's because human beings are *worth* recognizing.

Because the individual who is knowable through each body is so entirely *worth* being seen, and heard, and known and loved, God went to all the trouble of making every one of us different—billions of us, in fact—so that each one of us could be recognized by one another. Precisely because that *is* a lot of trouble, I have to believe that God had a pretty good reason for doing that purposeful cumbersome thing.

SAMENESS

Every human being has been made *distinct*—by height and hue and hair, by features and furrows and follicles—so that we can be recognized. It's *that* important.

If we were all robots, without our own thoughts and feelings, I suppose there wouldn't be any good reason we *shouldn't* all match. God could have created humankind like the robins or the clownfish, each one looking pretty much like the next. At that point we might as well all look like Beyoncé or Lucy Liu or Angelina Jolie or whoever is on the cover of *People* magazine this week.

Worse yet, what if each of us *were* unique on the inside, but we still all looked like Angelina on the outside? Were this the case, my husband, Peter, wouldn't have been able to find me splashing around in the pool at the bottom of the water park mountain because I'd have been looking so hot like all the other Angelinas. If I'd bought my floral-patterned bathing suit at Walmart, he would have been completely out of luck; there was a whole sea of those. I suppose, though, that since I can't walk barefoot because of my injured feet, he would have had a little advantage. He might have been able to press his face to the warm sticky pavement to look for the woman wearing one lime Croc and one purple one. So there's one nice thing about chronic injury. But what a *hassle*, right?!

Or what if every man looked like Brad Pitt? I understand that, for the briefest moment, this may sound more than a wee bit appealing. But I would also wager a guess that if every man looked like Brad Pitt, it might be a little less thrilling than it is right now. And, of course, if every man at the water park looked like Brad, I'd have to come up with some other fantastically clever way to find my barefoot husband when the park closed.

From a purely utilitarian perspective, the best thing I'd probably be able to come up with would be to clip a sign on his head or tattoo him some place really obvious so that I'd be able to recognize him from a distance. Because I'm an artist, I've actually given this a bit of thought. Some distinct indicator would need to be featured on some prominent body real estate, so that it didn't get lost among the crowded shuffle of knees and elbows. An armpit tattoo, for instance, would be totally useless. Something I could see while standing on a park bench would be optimal. I'd need to use bold shapes that could be recognized from forty or fifty feet. I'd want to employ unique colors. Something three-dimensional would even be better than the head sign.

At the end of the day, the most efficient solution I can dream of is pretty much what God's already got going with heads and faces right now. Distinct outlines, shapes, features and hues already allow us to recognize our loved ones.

Each one of us has been created unique because we are *worth* recognizing.

Ways Your Friends and Relatives
Probably Pick You Out in a Crowd

1. *Your height*

2. *Your girth*

3. *Your hair color*

4. *Your hairstyle*

5. *Your skin tone*

6. *Your face shape*

7. *Your facial features*

8. *Your gait*

9. *Your outfit*

10. *Your accessories*

UNRECOGNIZABLE

This very thing—the difficulty with distinguishing people—is also what's a little bit sinister about what happens in the fashion and beauty industry. Every day, somewhere, a woman walks into a plastic surgeon's office clutching a picture of Angelina or Lucy or Beyoncé. She hands the doctor a blown-up copy of one of their body parts that she'd like hers to match. Whether she wants hers to be made smaller, or bigger, or straighter, or smoother, or darker, or lighter, or thinner, or fuller, the fact is that she wants to look like someone else. No one is walking into these places begging to look like a Cyclops or to have follicles implanted in their faces that grow shaggy blue hair. The truth is that we don't really want to look *unique*. We can already do that for free. What we really want is to look similar to a physically attractive someone else. (Although I'm familiar with the "better version of myself" argument, I'm just not buyin' it.)

When an acquaintance of mine experienced sudden success as an international fashion model, I was itchy to browse through the magazines in which she appeared. I stood eagerly at Barnes & Noble, turning page after page after page, searching for her. Kylene is lanky and slender. Big eyes. Nice bone structure. Can you see where this is headed? I never found her. Although I squinted and stared, stared and squinted, I could never quite decide whether or not a particular model was the person I knew. Between the clothes, the makeup and the airbrushing, I was never sure whether or not I actually saw my friend. Although most people aren't complaining about this current situation, something about it is just not quite right.

Homogeneity sells. Business thrives, in fact, when women are made to appear other than they actually are. I'm not talking just about supermodels, either. When an ugly duckling normalish woman gets made over and transformed into a swan, in a magazine or on television, we celebrate her transformation—the loss of her actual, unique face—as an agreed-upon moral good. Am I the only one troubled by this weird phenomenon?

When people become unrecognizable—when they don't look like themselves—because they've been made over, or because they're chronically ill, or violently bruised, or dangerously burned, or morbidly obese, or surgically altered, or painfully thin, or digitally retouched, something is wrong. We were *made* to be recognized. If you can't find your friend in a magazine or at the bottom of a waterslide, something is wrong.

NOW

For me, this radical new insight put the current face and body situation into perspective. When I actually do lose track of Peter at the water park, I stand on a bench, scanning the crowds for the man I married. Seventy-five yards away I see a large, hulking figure with short dark hair pressing through the crowds in my direction. I squint to see a fuzzy image coming closer into view. Black hair, broad shoulders, orange suit: seems like it could be him. As he gets closer I make out the general shape of his head. Then the outline of his large eyes, nose and mouth comes into view. *Yup*, I confirm, satisfied, *it's him*.

I think that was God's whole thinking with the package design. From almost a hundred yards away we can gather enough information—from the size, shape, hair and gait—to make a pretty good guess that someone belongs to us. By *belonging* I don't mean that we have to wear matching team jerseys, enjoy the same ethnic dishes or display the same political signs in our yards. I just mean that, from someone's body—from her appearance—we can identify her as our daughter, or friend, or aunt, or sister-in-law, or neighbor. Scanning the face which has been so conveniently installed for display at the top of each person—which, in my opinion, is fantastic product design—most of us can make a positive ID from seventy yards or seven inches. The way God's got it set up, we can locate the people who are ours at airports, and football games and graduations and water parks.

TWIN LOBBYISTS

For a while I felt nervous that if I made a big deal about how important it is to be recognized as unique, I'd have a big problem with some fiery, identical-twin political action group. I was worried that I would say something offensive about how important it is for people to have unique, recognizable features, and then these imaginary twin lobbyists would be all over me.

Curious, I asked a friend with twin daughters about their distinguishing features. She told me about a little five-year-old friend of theirs who loves them but who can't tell them apart until he knows which outfit each one is wearing for the day. Until he does, he just goes about his playing business and addresses each one as "Twin."

This absolutely infuriates them.

That's when it hit me. Those twin activists wouldn't boycott me for saying that each person needs to be recognized as unique; they'd throw a stinkin' parade! After years of acquaintances and neighbors and church members sort of smiling vacantly at them, searching for which name to use and in the end never calling them by name, the twins—above all others—understand what I'm saying. *Everyone* deserves to be recognized, seen, heard, known, loved.

When you *can* identify someone you know and love—from the shape of her silhouette, or the vivacious kink of her hair, or the jaunt in her gait, or the mole near her chin, or the curve of her jaw—something is right.

Simply put: because we were *made* to be loved, we were also made to be recognized. These bodies have been given for the purpose of relationship. For my two cents, the uniqueness of every person is a brilliant plan on God's part. Just brilliant.

It's just too bad we're not better sports about the whole thing.

12

FUNCTION

JD's Fabulous Breasts
and Other Useful Body Parts

A few years ago I asked a bunch of friends, "If you could change *one thing* about your body, what would it be?"

Take a moment to think about it, friend, before you read further.

The results were pretty much what I expected. Discretely folded index cards revealed a few dimply thighs, an under-appreciated nose, some curvy butts and a bunch of cellulite. When I've repeated this little party trick in other groups, I have typically gotten about the same results. We are concerned about how our bodies appear.

Duh.

What makes these concerns *remarkable*, in my book, is that not one person I surveyed mentioned wanting to change anything about the way her body *worked*. For instance, one woman in the group had a bad back. One needed knee surgery. Another lived with a chronic disease. Are you with me? We have been conditioned to care more about how our bodies look than about how they function. We say we don't, but a lot of us really do.

This is insanity, people. It's like a person who's starving to death walking into a grocery store with a wad of cash for food and drink and coming out having purchased scented nail polish and a big, shiny Mylar balloon.

I can only speak for the weird twisted things that happen in my own heart but, without precise calculations, I would venture a guess that I've probably spent more time longing for large beautiful eyes with thick lashes behind my stylish glasses than I have spent longing for vision that would negate the need for the glasses. I've paid more money for bras that promise to hold my breasts at just the right altitude than I've donated to breast cancer research. I've spent more energy thinking about, shopping for and decorating some of my fabulous shoes than I have spent praying that my chronically injured feet—let alone those of others—would be healed. I've been more concerned with eliminating the curvy curves around my middle than I have been about eliminating poverty in the lives of thin, bony children around the globe, and in my neighborhood, who live daily with hunger and malnutrition.

And I don't even look that good.

Our culture has thoroughly and effectively marketed the myth that women's bodies exist for no higher purpose than to be *viewed*. Most of us aren't even aware how deeply the message has invaded our hearts. We're pretty much okay with the fact that painfully stylish high heels, making our legs appear longer and sexier, are causing permanent injury to our feet. With the notable exception of those who have bad backs, a lot of us don't really *know* what abdominal muscles actually *do*, when they're not being ogled on bare bellies. We pour millions of dollars into hair products so that our hairs will appear different, to others, instead of letting them poke out of our heads naturally. And we are simply not horrified *enough* when parents buy their daughters breast implants for their Sweet Sixteen. As if we have no awareness that we've been made to walk with the Lord in a vibrant, living relationship of love and service, we live, and eat, and shop, and dress as if our bodies were meant for the visual enjoyment of others.

If you think I'm making this up, just take a peek in your closet. On the floor. At your shoes. The ones you wear to weddings. Nothing good can come from most of those injurious death-traps. You know it's true. In my opinion, anything that has to be *removed* from one's body to celebrate a friend's wedding by doing the Electric Slide or the Cupid Shuffle isn't worth owning.

This is all I'm saying.

JEAN BUTTS

I'm not pretending that I've never found myself in this tempting situation of treating my body as ornamental rather than instrumental. It's not as if I've never painfully contorted the upper half of my body in order to twist around to glimpse my butt in a full-length mirror to monitor how it looks in jeans. And really: what's that even about?

As we purpose to distinguish between valuing the *appearance* of our bodies and valuing their *function*, this is where the rubber hits the road. The butt-checking, I mean. What on earth are we confirming, in the Marshalls dressing room or in the privacy of our own bedrooms, when we turn around and peek to see how our butts look? It's not like *we* have to look at them when we're out at the movies or in a restaurant or at the mall. So really, we're taking a long, hard look at the body part whose most important job is sitting, and we're trying to decide what a stranger or a clerk or a loved one will think or experience when he or she happens to glance at the pockets of our loose or snug Levi's.

When I've done this, I didn't even know what I was hoping for. Did I want someone to admire it? Desire it? Reach out and touch it?

Though I really can't answer that, I realize now that I had decided—if you can call it that—that the judgment of others mattered to me.

I understand now that this is cuckoo behavior.

WRINKLES AND FURROWS AND SPOTS

I'm not proud of my butt-checking moments. On some days, though, I do live into the freedom of valuing the body God gave me for what it can do; on those days, I don't give my butt a second thought. In fact, not only am I willing to overlook my various aesthetic faux pas, but in the name of function, I have actually come to embrace them.

For instance, one of my favorite things in the world to do is to walk at the beach on a warm, sunny day. For depression and other assorted afflictions, it is definitely my drug of choice. Who can stay bummed out for long when they get to walk across green grass and golden sand, under blue skies, past purple and orange and turquoise houses? Typically, not me.

As I wind through the crowded boardwalk at Venice Beach, outside Los Angeles, my eyes squint against the rising midday sun. Since my stepdad is an ophthalmologist, I live with a nagging sense of guilt about the fact that I don't wear sunglasses; I've just never been able to make them work for me. I tried the dark plastic shield that goes over regular eyeglasses, but I felt like my grandfather. I tried some round, purple clip-on ones, but they made me feel like John Lennon. And though I do have the means to spring for a pair of prescription sunglasses, I never have. As I pass vendors and sand sculptors and the lady who paints your name on a grain of rice, I begin to reconsider the wisdom of not wearing them.

In pensive moments like this, I invariably find myself thinking about cavemen and cavewomen. I do. Surely, I tell myself, the cave people got along without plastic sunglasses. In fact, I convince myself that, in the face of the blazing sun, cave people probably did what I do: they squinted. Squinting against the bright sun is probably why God invented squinty muscles in the first place. That's what I tell myself.

When I get back to my mom and stepfather's home, after a few hours outside, I glance in the mirror. Because the sun draws out my freckles, the blotchy skin on my face is like my own personal mood ring. Moving closer to the mirror, I happen to notice that a few of the freckles have accidentally clumped together. Then I realize that there are several patches like that. Without warning, the angst-ridden voice in a commercial from my childhood rings in my head: "They call these *age spots*. I call them ugly. But what's a woman to do?" Though I vaguely recall that a woman was supposed to buy some product, I forget now what it was.

It isn't just the spots that are advertising my aging situation; I also notice two deep lines between my eyebrows. Those lines suggest that, like some brilliant scientist, I've been thinking incredibly profound thoughts for the last several decades—even though I haven't. The lines are just from all the squinting.

Truly, I am a beauty consultant's nightmare. After all, if I'd worn a big floppy sun hat for decades, plus whatever cream my consultant was selling, I might not have all those age spots. If I had used sunglasses, there wouldn't be the deep lines from all the squinting. If I hadn't *smiled* so much about all the gorgeous colors at the beach—if I'd been stone-faced and nonplussed and entirely unimpressed with all that natural and painted beauty—I wouldn't have such deep *smile lines* around my mouth. If I'd been sensible and avoided all that great stuff, I'd probably look younger and a lot less worn than I do now.

Yuck, right?

Who even wants to live like that??! If I have to choose between the spotty wrinkles and a lifetime of looking at a dulled-down sunglasses version of turquoise houses and bright purple doors and neon orange stucco, give me the wrinkles! I want to squint and smile at gorgeous colors and—with proper UV protection— feel the warm sunshine melting my freckles together into unsightly age spots. That other second-rate show—the dulled-down one—is kind of what life is like when we get so obsessed with how our bodies appear that we forget that they were made for living—for splashing, walking, serving, smiling and squinting.

I may not be thinking clearly because I'm all hopped up on sunshine at this very moment. I will speculate, though, that God intentionally *gave* an extra measure of sunshine at the beach precisely so we wouldn't waste so much time worrying about our dimply thighs and bulgy stomachs and too-small or too-big boobs sagging toward earth in our bathing suits. This is my personal theory. Though Scripture gives no indication that this reasoning was part of God's master plan, Jesus' Father was all about setting people free. Even when the thing by which we're bound is a twisted preoccupation with self.

JD

I am particularly inspired to live differently by other women who use their bodies to do the kind of stuff God made them to do. I'm thinking about women who wield a scalpel to perform life-saving surgeries. Or there are the ones who hold and rock and caress drug-addicted infants who were born to addicted mothers. Women who till the soil in their yards, kneeling to plant vegetables to feed their family and others, use their bodies well. So do ones who wiggle a paintbrush or knitting needles to fashion fabulous creations. I'm thinking about dancing women who step and tap and pop and lock, or women in the Peace Corps who dig wells and teach other women how to raise and milk goats. The composite collage of these women—their hands and knees and calves and biceps—reminds me what bodies are for.

My friend JD is a woman like this. I really, *really* want to tell you about JD, even though, as a rule, I try not to employ exotic stories about missionaries living deep in the heart of Africa as examples of faithful Christian living. I've got nothing against these people, per se; it's just that it's too easy for most of us normal women and girls to write off their super-Christian heroics as being irrelevant to our daily lives in the suburbs. I'm about to break my rule with the express request that you not write off this particular African missionary as a super-Christian. I promise you she puts on her flip-flops one at a time, just like the rest of us.

JD and her husband, Kevin, had heard God's call to serve among a remote and primitive people in Bundibugyo, Uganda (pronounced Bun-dah-BOO-jee-yo—which, it turns out, is pretty fun to say). Bundibugyo, an extremely impoverished region, was without electricity, running water and any written language. When Jesus sent his disciples to "the ends of the earth," I'm pretty sure he was thinking about Bundibugyo.

Within a few years, JD and Kevin were raising a baby and a toddler in the heart of Africa. Since no infant formula was available, and because JD was the one with the actual breasts, the lion's share of the child nurture fell to her. Having to cook everything from scratch, sans labor-saving devices, she explains that she was under no illusion that she "had a life outside of the kitchen." "I thought back over all of the missionary adventure novels I'd read in college," she says, "and for the life of me I couldn't remember any that described a mom's life on the field. When I thought about being a missionary like Jim Elliot, I did not think about making hundreds of loaves of bread. I wanted to *be* a missionary, not just married to one."

Like so many other women around the globe, the frustrated mother of an infant and toddler reasoned with God, "Lord, could you give me something *significant* to do? I spend most of my time breastfeeding and scrubbing out poopy cloth diapers. I want something more."

Soon after this cry to heaven, JD and her friend Karen learned that a nearby woman had been shot and killed by rebels while working in her garden. Miraculously, the three-month-old baby who had been tied to the slain woman's back had survived. Typically, in this culture, when a mother died in childbirth, the common custom was to lay the baby's body beside the mother's and wait for death. The next morning both could be buried together. Other wives or aunts were frightened to provide care for these infants because of the prevalent belief in witchcraft and fear of the spiritual world. They feared that the curse would also infect them or their children. Because this particular baby's father and grandmothers had grown so attached to this little girl, though, they brought her to the mission compound begging for help. They had absolutely no way to feed baby Kobu.

At the time, JD and Karen were both nursing their own infants. When they heard the news, they exchanged a look between them that said, "Got milk!" With a twinkle in her eye, JD points to the grace of that moment, explaining, "The gift of *not* being Jim Elliot was great." When the two friends had nursed Kobu for five months, they visited her family to discuss the process of returning the chubby, smiley baby to her grandmothers. Most neighbors in the family's village, originally assuming the baby had been cursed, couldn't believe that Kobu was still alive and thriving.

"Word spread like wildfire—not only throughout our district but into eastern Congo as well," JD explains. "Before we knew it, families were bringing us tiny babies, hours old, whose mothers had died in childbirth." JD and her friend began by providing foster care and nursing these precious newborns. As the need increased, the two women began researching types of milking goats. JD and Karen started teaching families to strain and boil a goat's milk, adjusting the amount of water used depending on the baby's age and weight. Every week the women would meet with grandmothers to encourage them, offer them a little pocket money, weigh the babies and ensure that the infants were getting any medical care they needed. After a year in the program, these families graduated. Today hundreds of these chubby toddlers, otherwise destined to perish, are waddling around Bundibugyo.

Now of course, when I see JD when she is home on furlough, I can't help but marvel at her wonderful chest. I have to believe that JD and those heavily-sucked paps are celebrated royalty in a culture that values kingdom priorities. And once again, I'd like to express my regret about telling a story about missionaries deep in the heart of Africa, but it was sort of important. Magazines like

Playboy, shows like *Desperate Housewives* and restaurants like Hooters have made it necessary to take you seventy-two thousand miles from here to glimpse some truly amazing breasts.

THANKFULLY

Thankfully, you probably don't have to go that far to see women's bodies that have been spent for others. Fairly close to home you probably can find once-six-packed abs which have, after bearing babies, devolved into saggy, stretch-marked bellies that no one likes to show off at the beach anymore. You can also glimpse some wonderfully roundish bellies that haven't borne humans, but have simply eaten one too many pastries over coffee while listening to friends. You can see thick thighs squatting to gather backyard eggs to share with neighbors. Keep an eye open for aunts of toddlers whose jeans are worn through at the knees from playing on the floor. Notice wide bottoms of older women, on neighborhood porches and tucked away in nursing homes, who pray for those in need of prayer.

So there's something nice and convenient.

Though most of the messages we receive every day scream otherwise, the purpose of bodies is not to appear attractive to others. They were made to do stuff and to be in relationship with others. Feet were made to dance the Electric Slide, eyes were made to see fabulous colors, breasts were made to feed babies, and butts were made for sitting.

Once we truly believe this, deep in our bones, we're finally liberated for life that really is life.

13

CELEBRATION

Embracing Our Queenliness

My family was playing Sorry on our front porch a few weeks ago when our neighbor Ivy drove by, waving to us. Rather than passing by, though, she stopped her car and climbed the few steps up to our porch. I was thrilled, and sort of felt like a celebrity had stopped by. She's not a celebrity, but she does have a full life, loving lots of people. I think this is why the visit felt extraspecial.

I quickly glanced around our messy porch to find her the best seat in the house. Said seat happened to be a hand-carved, red velvet wooden throne. We actually put it on the porch a few months ago in hopes that it would get stolen, but it never was. I'm sort of glad, because now it's really grown on me.

Motioning with my arm, I insisted, "Please, sit on the throne!"

Without missing a beat, Ivy agreed: "A throne for an African queen!"

Because I know she's a social worker, and not royalty from the actual continent of Africa, I wasn't sure, at first, what she meant by African queen.

Maybe it was her hair. As she dropped into her throne, my daughter Zoë and I marveled at Ivy's styled black hair, braided and twisted in swooping locks. Perhaps that was the royal reference. I could easily imagine a queen wearing that beautiful style.

As we chatted, I also eyed her fabulous jewelry, wondering if that could be the distinguishing queenly factor. Coolly, I commented, "I love your necklace."

"It's Nepalese," she explained.

Rats! Everyone knows African queens wear authentic African jewelry.

I wondered quietly to myself, if it wasn't the actual job description, or the hair, or the jewelry, then what *made* her an African queen?

As the conversation continued, I slowly figured it out. No friend of low self-esteem, Ivy simply sees herself as precious and beautiful and beloved. Believe me, if I could bottle that stuff, I'd include a vial with every copy of this book.

SELF-EXPRESSION

Ivy and I chatted a little bit about beauty. Specifically, I mentioned how super-duper-unimportant appearance is, and that what really matters is that God gave us bodies for loving God and loving others the way we love ourselves. I was certain that my progressive, spiritually minded friend would nod in agreement with that big brilliant idea.

And while she didn't exactly *not* agree with me, I realized that our neighborhood African queen seemed to know something else about bodies, something to which I'd been squeezing my eyes shut.

"Bodies," announced Ivy with a huge grin, "are for *expressing* ourselves!"

Although I wasn't prepared to swallow it whole, something about Ivy's affirmation sounded sort of . . . right.

"Hmmm . . ." I mused. Curious, I prompted, "Say some more about that."

"We express ourselves," she continued, "in how we dress, and how we decorate ourselves and how we carry ourselves."

The moment it was out there, I did not *want* to agree with that statement. In fact I resist, absolutely resist—I mean kicking and screaming—buying into this sort of thinking that places even the teeniest value on appearances. It's not even a resistance to *buying into*, really, as much as . . . *acknowledging* that appearances could possibly be just a little bit meaningful.[1]

"Crabby Margot, are you saying that we should all be walking around with pasty skin, limp hair and circles under our eyes, wearing colorless clothes and sensible shoes? I can't imagine that when Jesus said he came to give life in abundance, he could have had an entirely light tan wardrobe in mind. Margot, are you for real?"

Yes, I am for real, but I'm not saying that dull lifeless thing. I'm not asking any woman to stock her closet with a single beige garment to be worn day in and day out. (Unless you're a zookeeper.)

I can easily see how it might seem hypocritical for me to pretend that I don't care a whit about appearances, when I kind of do. I was actually made aware of this disturbing hypocrisy situation when more than one sharp thinker pointed it out to me recently. I really had to wrestle with this to figure out what my big problem was with recognizing any sort of value in appearances. Finally, it came.

I realized that the simplicity-loving part of me lives in conflict—or perhaps a healthy tension—with the beauty-loving part. I just do not want to lend my endorsement to a philosophy of the body, like dressing and decorating, that requires something to be *purchased*. Yuck. As I settled down and listened closely, though, my neighbor Ivy wasn't saying that an individual's worth was contingent upon the available credit limit on her Nordstrom charge card. She was just saying that we *express* ourselves in the

---

[1] I'm willing to entertain the remote possibility that I've gone a little overboard and may need to dial it back a hair. Or two. Or possibly an entire hairdo.

way we present our bodies. Which, I could admit, we do.

It wasn't just the simplicity-loving part of me that was reticent about celebrating appearances; it was the *realist* part. Plenty of precious women, entirely beloved by God and others, simply won't fit into a mold that is recognizable, by fallen human eyes, as "physically beautiful." The gospel fact is that people who live with facial disfigurement, or other atypical conditions, have an inherent value that simply *must* be dissociated from our human perceptions of physical attractiveness. This really gets me pretty fired up. But Ivy wasn't saying anyone's value was predicated on looking like a Cover Girl. She was simply saying that we express who we are in how we present ourselves.

Possibly, I grudgingly allowed, she wasn't as extra-wrong as I hoped she might be.

Ten Occasions When a Woman Might Choose to Put Some Energy into Her Appearance

1. *If your style—maybe your nose ring or your tattoos or your tongue piercing—really bothers your mother, dress up for her fiftieth birthday party like an American Girl doll. (Been there, done that.)*

2. *If you've cut off your pretty long hair to donate to Locks of Love, an organization that makes wigs for those who have lost their hair to cancer treatments, spruce your short hair up. Don't let it look like sad, grieving, recently truncated hair. Consider spiky gel.*

3. *If you're going shoeless for a day in order to raise awareness about children around the globe who suffer for want of shoes, paint your toenails. Look jazzy. Start conversations.*

4. *If you're fasting, style your hair and freshen your makeup. Since these things are best done in secret, don't let anyone figure it out!*

5. If you visit a congregation or office or family in which formal dress is expected, you can honor your host with your dress.

6. If you're an attorney for International Justice Mission, prosecuting a case of human trafficking, don't go casual. Show 'em you mean business.

7. When you visit your grandparents' fancy nursing home and join them in the dining hall for dinner, pick something from your wardrobe that approximates what they'll be wearing.

8. If you've had a mastectomy, and are planning reconstructive surgery or looking for a bathing suit with fake, squishy breasts, just go crazy and choose the perkiest new breasts you can find. Really live it up.

9. If you're getting married and your groom enjoys henna art, invite your friends to decorate your back with beautiful designs.

10. If you're involved with a ministry or summer camp for kids or teens, and you're going to open the day with a skit, please pull out all the stops when you costume yourself as a banana or a caveman or a space cowgirl. Really dress to impress.

TRUENESS

Clearly, in fashion as with food, my growing edge is to find some middle ground. Because even though I'm reluctant to admit it, there *is* something about our outsides that reflects who we are inside. It doesn't have to be a huge diamond ring or pricey evening gown. The way we present ourselves, groom ourselves, carry ourselves and dress ourselves often *does* indicate to others something about us.

I get this. If I have to wear anything dressy that requires heels or hose, I usually want to pin a sign to my bejeweled bosom that reads: "The woman standing in front of you is not the real Margot. She is an impostor."

On the other hand, there are also ways I present myself that make me feel like I am being *exactly* who God made me to be. I really do love to look as bright as a jazzy wildflower. I enjoy expressing who I am—precious and beloved and God-made and alive—in the way I dress. Most often these happy moments involve brightly colored comfortable clothes, a homemade rainbow necklace, stripy socks and daisy-painted, steel-toed work boots. Though I probably look more jesterly than queenly, I *feel* like a queen. I think that shows.

In the end, I suspect Ivy is probably just more *honest* about appearances than I am. There *is* something particular about how we hold our heads, and move our bodies, and clothe them, and decorate them that reflects what is *true* about us.

Like my happy-walking, the trueness doesn't have to be the kind of blinding wildflower sort of true that I enjoy. The way we dress might say, "I celebrate my femininity," or it could say, "I'm more comfortable keeping my figure under looser wraps." The way we decorate ourselves might say, "I am a carnival on legs!" It might also say, "I'd prefer not to draw too much attention to myself." The way we carry ourselves could say, "I've been hurt and I'd rather move through the world a little more protected," or it could shout, "I really like who God has made me to be." After my period of reflection, I began to reluctantly entertain the possibility that appearances might be a teeny-weeny little bit meaningful.

As I did, I recalled that when I traveled outside of affluent America, to India and Africa, some of the poorest women *did* express themselves through the colorful garments they wore. My friend Phileena, who travels the globe to be among the poorest of the poor, explains, "A poor woman in India, not sure where her next meal will come from, takes dignity in her appearance and femininity, gracing her body with a colorful sari and her hair with a garland of flowers." I know that Phileena is right. Even these poor ones find the proud wherewithal to pound their bright colorful garments cleaner and brighter than mine have ever been.

They wrap themselves in radiant patterns and hold their heads high. Without the privilege of credit cards or layaway, they allow their outsides to reflect what is true about their precious insides.

As I began to think about brilliant Native American regalia and colorful South American jewelry, I couldn't help but speculate that this kind of creative embellishment must surely spring from the same sort of impulse that led to the Creator's exotic painting of flowers and rainbows and poisonous dark frogs. The brilliant colors in Guatemalan weaving and African kente cloth aren't about hiding anything, or disguising it. They're about making what already is—a unique cultural beauty—apparent.

So since there doesn't seem to be an extra charge for beautiful color, and since it's free to throw your shoulders back and to swoop your hair up proudly and to garnish yourself with bright roadside vegetation, I will reluctantly, honestly admit that possibly appearances might mean a little something. In rejecting the world's rigid, narrow, strangling mold of beauty, I suppose there's no good reason to throw the beauty out with the bathwater.

I'm now willing to concede that there are probably worse things than having our outsides project the inside truth of knowing that we are precious and beautiful and beloved.

Probably.

14

NEED-MEETING

The Life-Changing Day
I Actually *Needed* a Milkshake

When my kids whine for something they want, the very last thing I want to do is to give them whatever they're whining about. If this is a Star Wars LEGO Republic Attack Gunship, we're probably all better off because of my naturally lazy and irritable demeanor. When they're whining because they're hungry, even though I just fed them, I really do have to learn how to be a little more flexible.

It is so good I'm not God.

When God's people trekked across the desert wilderness, they whined because they missed the burgers they used to get at BK, back in Egypt. God, however, more gracious than I, used the opportunity to teach the Israelites about God's own inherent trustworthiness. God sent quail in the evenings for dinner, and decided to rain down actual bread from heaven each morning to feed them. I can't help but think that if I had that magic little number in my bag of tricks, I might not be so impatient about going back and forth to the kitchen to slice up more carrots or apples.

FANTASTIC

Well, God's children thought that meat and bread that magically appeared out of nowhere was just fantastic. Who wouldn't? Instructed to gather as much as they needed, they ate it off the ground, they scooped it into cloths and tied it up in hobo sacks, and they even stuffed it in their pockets. They just went nuts. The next day, however, the extra bread they'd gathered and not eaten had maggots. Nasty, huh?

These, though, were holy maggots. I know that sounds like an oxymoron, or something Robin would exclaim to Batman in astonishment. The whole point of the instructive crawling larvae though, was that God wanted to teach his people to trust him enough to provide for their needs every day. By taking just as much as they needed for the day, the children of God would learn to live out their trust in God. They learned it with their bodies.

So many of the Old Testament laws involved a bodily response—eating kosher, burying quickly, sacrificing doves. Just look at the Ten Commandments. The big ten, as dictated to Moses, turned out to be *mostly* about the particular movements of hands and knees and tongues and other body parts. Hands aren't for making idols or stealing stuff or murdering, knees aren't for worshiping idols, tongues aren't for lying or taking God's name in vain, and bodies—in general—aren't made for working on the sabbath or committing adultery. That still leaves a lot of other stuff bodies *can* do, but those are the ones that are off-limits. What we do with our bodies matters to God. Israel *got* that. Today we're called into the same kind of living, bodily relationship.

I'm not saying that God is stocking the Arizona desert with quail or raining down corn flakes from heaven. In fact, if God were, I'm not even convinced that we'd go out and collect them. I can easily imagine that slothful scenario.

Today, though, we *are* still invited to express our trust in, and dependence upon, God by gathering just what we need. When we use the resources God has given us for our daily bread, to buy what we need, drink what we need, eat what we need and wear what we need, we still express our trust in and dependence upon a God who provides. I realize this measured dependence is a pretty hard concept for a lot of us to grasp, especially those of us who are accustomed to flashing plastic cards that get us into Costco or Sam's Club, where we routinely buy obscene amounts of salty snacks and mega-count tampons.

We have been invited to enter deeply into a bodily relationship, not *just* a spiritual or cerebral one, with God. We honor this relationship when we're out gathering at the grocery store or the clothing store or the strip mall, and—like the Israelites wandering in the wilderness—we gather just what we need. If we have the shoes we need to protect our bodies at home, at school, at work, we express our trust in a good Provider by not buying more shoes. When we have the food we need to survive and thrive, we don't buy more food. Like I said, this is a pretty hard concept around which to wrap our minds. Even if we do understand it, intellectually, putting it into practice takes some real concerted effort. I never cease to find this absurd. While billions are working desperately to acquire what they need for survival, I have to put forth actual effort to *not* acquire stuff.

Too often those of us who are over-resourced fail at this very thing, thereby breaking relationship with God and others. I know this is true because when I have failed to trust in God with my own gathering—when I over-shop and hoard and leave cereal boxes open and waste food by throwing it in the garbage—the wrath of God has actually been manifest in my very own kitchen. That's right: we get varmints. *Holy cockroaches, Batman! Find the mouse traps!* It's sort of hard to miss the similarities between the

Israelites in the desert and that yucky consequence.

Too many of us live without any clear discernment between need and want.

QUARRY

Last summer I was being very regimented about avoiding desserts of all varieties. Like I said, I don't think it was the best way to live, but it was a wee bit better than the recurring, physically unhealthy alternative.

It was a Sunday afternoon, and our family had decided to go swimming at the local quarry. Though my husband and I love this fun adventure, we usually have to bribe our three children to coerce them into being less crabby about it than they'd naturally be. I need to mention that on one of these adventures, when we thoughtlessly scheduled the food bribe to occur *after* the hike and swim combo, we came perilously close to losing a child to death-by-crabbiness. And possibly one adult. It didn't take more than once to learn that the bribe needed to happen *before* the fun shenanigans.

The next outing, after donning swimsuits and flip-flops and gathering towels and hats and inner tubes and water bottles, we were finally ready to leave. In all the flurry of the gathering the stuff, however, I didn't calculate the last time I'd eaten. As we pulled away from home, I realized it had been quite awhile.

I knew Peter had plans to stop on the way to the quarry to get some amazing milkshake bribes for the children and for himself. As we drove, I realized that I was looking at a one-mile hike through the woods to the quarry, then jumping and splashing and swimming and floating for who knows how long, hiking back out again and driving fifteen minutes home. Because I have a little history of fainting, I worried I might not make it without some sort of sustenance.

The fuzzy-voiced cashier was taking Peter's order through the drive-thru speaker when, impulsively, I told Peter to order one more. Cookies and cream. His wide eyes belied his surprise.

"Food emergency," I grunted in explanation.

Fearful that I wouldn't survive a few more hours without food, I honestly had myself whipped into such a frenzy about it that it truly *did* feel like an emergency. As I was waiting for the milkshake, I suddenly became aware of something that I probably should have known a lot sooner.

Food is fuel.

I know that sounds like some ancient Schoolhouse Rock jingle, or the title of a middle-school nutrition textbook, but somehow the fact hit me in an entirely new way in that moment. I suddenly knew, in my deepest places, that on that particular afternoon, there was something entirely *right* about enjoying the good gift of that milkshake before plunging into the great outdoors with my family. I have never felt more wonderful about drinking a sweet, fatty milkshake in my life. I exercised regularly, I was in actual need of food, and all the fat and calories would give me energy to walk and carry the kids' stuff and swim and, like the others, probably be even less crabby than I would otherwise be. I now think of that lap through the drivethru as the Modern-Day Milkshake Miracle. Seriously, that milkshake changed my life.

It's important to note, of course, that food is *also* about more than fuel. In Scripture it's given to bless, given for celebration and given for fellowship. I am simply rejoicing about the fuel part because, among those of us who are affluent, it's much too easily forgotten.

If, like me, you've had weird, ongoing situations with iceberg lettuce or cheesy pizza, this is really a concept you want to grasp. Though some of us use food to soothe and manage our emotions, and drink drinks to wake us up, calm us down or knock us out, food and drink were meant to nourish and fuel our bodies.

It was the plan.

It's no coincidence that, to this day, some of my best eating moments have been when my body actually needs food to do something fantastic, like swim in the quarry, hike across town or go on a long bike ride to surprise old friends with a visit.

It's just . . . right.

DEPENDABILITY

This is why Jesus really knocked himself out trying to convince his friends that his Father was dependable. I don't think it's any coincidence that Jesus' two big themes in his address about trusting our Father were clothing and food. The appropriate care of and provision for our bodies, whether impoverished or affluent, is the precise place where Jesus invites us to trust God.

If God feeds the birds, Jesus asks, won't he feed you? If God clothed the flowers so beautifully, Jesus had argued, can't you trust that he'll clothe you too? He could have been speaking directly to me. Or you. "What I'm trying to do here," says Jesus, "is get you to relax, not be so preoccupied with getting so you can respond to God's giving. . . . You'll find all your everyday human concerns will be met. Don't be afraid of missing out" (Luke 12:29 *The Message*).

"Not being so preoccupied with getting" is harder than it looks.

Jesus recognized that trusting God for what we need was a pretty big challenge for first-century disciples. Strangely, nothing has changed for twenty-first-century ones. Both the affluent and the underprivileged are challenged when it comes to trusting God with our everyday needs.

At the root of this human clawing for more food, clothes and stuff is fear. We have, at our core, an innate concern about receiving both the provision and the nurture we need and crave. Though we may not even be aware of it, we live with a deep, gnawing anxiety that our needs for provision and nurture will not be met. So many of us scramble to stave off that neediness by filling our mouths, filling our closets, filling our homes, filling our bank accounts, filling our eyes, filling our minds or filling our bodies with whatever takes the edge off. We take more than we need so that we'll never be empty. We'll never hunger. So that we won't *really* have to trust in what God provides.

KINGDOM PRIORITIES

Though God longs for us to live into that trust, responsible stewardship with what's left over isn't just about us. It's about others. John the Baptist, who was out on the campaign trail stumping for Jesus in the wilderness, was the first guy to introduce the very radical nature of this whole thing.

"The man with two tunics," instructed John, "should share with him who has none, and the one who has food should do the same" (Luke 3:11). I am of the mind that most churchy people should be a little more shocked by this than we actually are.

At a seventieth birthday celebration for Tony Campolo, his sisters, Rose Holland and Ann Scull, shared a story about their brother's response to this passage as a child. Having heard the story in Sunday school, he had come home and started rifling through the closets. Pulling out coats, he allowed each family member just one.

"Look at all the coats we have!" Tony insisted. Then, gesturing toward his two sisters, Tony demanded, "How many are yours? And how many are yours? Do you know there are people right here in this country who don't even have *one* coat?!"

You've got to love this earnest little guy.

Tony's mother, the kind I'd like to be, finally agreed, "Okay, Tony. We'll get a bag and we'll fill it and we'll give it to the needy."

Don't you just love her too? Other adults might have just patted him on the head and thought to themselves, *Kids say the darnedest things!* Not Tony's mom. She *got* it. She understood that God provides for the poor through those who respond to God's giving, the ones who are willing to agree, "Enough *is* enough."

I hear similar strains in the prayer that Jesus taught his followers to pray. After all, he didn't instruct us to pray for caviar or Diet

Coke or Cheetos—all the stuff to which we pretty much assume we're entitled. Instead, he taught us to pray, "Give us this day our daily bread." It's sort of funny how we deduce, from that, that we're entitled to ask God for so much more stuff than the food and clothes we need to meet our daily needs.

Clearly, it's all very *un*-American.

15

ACCEPTANCE

Unfortunate Stereotypes
and the Lies We Believe

If I hadn't seen it with my own eyes, I wouldn't have believed it.

Long before I was ever hired as director of spiritual development at a north Jersey residential facility for folks living with disabilities, a crew of volunteers came in regularly to lead worship with the residents. Not long after I began, I was told to expect a deacon from a local Catholic church and his worship helper. These men, I was told, had been coming for years, on the second Sunday afternoon of each month, to minister to the residents.

If they'd told me a priest was coming, I'd have been able to imagine who to expect. I'd have waited in the facility's common room, glancing at my watch every few minutes, and kept an eye open for a nice old man wearing black shoes, black pants, a black shirt and white collar. He would have come into the building quietly, clutching a Bible, and then shuffled into the room, introduced himself, said some liturgical words, possibly felt a little uncomfortable and then gotten on his way. That's what I thought would probably happen.

The fact that I was, in fact, waiting for two Roman Catholic laypeople gave me no opportunity to mentally stereotype anyone before they arrived. Or so I thought.

When Jim Mueller and his friend Joe entered the building, I took one look at those guys and decided they probably weren't the worship leaders for whom I was waiting. I assumed they must be kindhearted Mafia uncles of one of our residents. But, dressed in trench coats and caps, one was hauling a guitar and the other was carrying a tote bag with what turned out to be songbooks. I realized they were there to lead the service. In an instant, these two middle-aged Italian men blew every category I'd had, until that moment, for worship leader. Not knowing exactly what was inside the guitar case didn't help.

Being such an astute observer of people and a snap-judger extraordinaire, I could tell, in one glance, which one was in charge and which one was the silent bodyguard who kept everyone in line. I introduced myself and learned that Jim, the head guy, was the deacon for whom I'd been waiting. His north Jersey Italian cadence did nothing to convince me I wouldn't have seen him on *The Sopranos* if we'd had cable television.

What came next would expose more than my disturbing prejudice about north Jersey Italian Catholics.

As the two men crossed the threshold into the community room, Jim's face lit up like fireworks. In a voice louder than any I'd ever heard in that building, he started shouting, "Hello, hello! Jesus loves you! Jesus loves you just the way you are! Isn't that wonderful? Hello friends, Jesus loves you just the way you are!" Laying his coat over his arm and still carrying the dubious guitar case, Jim wound his way through wheelchairs and kneelers and walkers and couches, gently touching every resident. "Jesus loves you just the way you are!" Everything about Jim's face and voice and body agreed with those eight bellowed words that still hung in the air throughout the building: "Jesus loves you just the way you are!"

He was like a loud, Catholic Mr. Rogers. Without the tennis shoes.

As Jim got settled in, the strong, silent bodyguard handed out songbooks to residents and family members and staff. Wanting to be useful and not look quite so shocked at what was transpiring before my eyes, I distributed some maracas and bells and tambourines.

The service continued for twenty or thirty minutes with songs and Bible stories. At its conclusion, Deacon Jim dipped an evergreen branch in what I think was holy water. Then he flicked it around the room so that some of the spray landed on everyone. Because I didn't know it was coming, I felt a little confused that he was flicking all of us without our consent. I didn't think I was being baptized, but I couldn't be entirely sure. During subsequent visits, once I'd finally realized it was some sort of blessing, I would always try to position myself next to a resident near the front so that I'd get a huge, full dose of it. Honestly, I couldn't get enough.

As the months went by, I decided that whatever Deacon Jim had, I wanted. Even though I didn't use a wheelchair or a computerized communication device or a hearing aid, I wanted to receive and live into the almost unbelievable message that Jesus really did love me just the way I was.

That first visit, though, everything inside me wanted to correct Deacon Jim. I wanted to protest in theological indignation, "Jesus doesn't love my sin!" That wasn't what Jim was saying, however. On behalf of my friends, I wanted to shout out, "Jesus doesn't delight in disability!" Of course, Jim wasn't saying that either. If I'd been completely honest, I might have hollered, "He might love my heart, but he certainly can't be thrilled with these hips!"

And yet, if I understood him correctly, Jesus loved me entirely, even with the hips.

What Jim was saying, loudly and repetitively, month in and

month out, year after year, was that Jesus really does love us as we are. I realize it's a hard message to swallow—much harder than the lies hissing that we're unacceptable as we are. Those are really easy to believe. To this day, I still work to wrap my mind around the big concept that even with all the imperfection, Jesus still loves us exactly as we are.

Pretty big, huh?

Lies That Are Really Easy to Believe

1. I'm not thin enough.

2. I'm not pretty enough.

3. I'm not tall enough.

4. I'm too tall.

5. I'm not curvy enough.

6. I'm too curvy.

7. I'm not the right color.

8. I'm not the right proportions.

9. I'm not "hot" enough.

10. I'm just not enough.

SCOTT

About this time I'd been emailing my brother, Scott. If memory serves, we'd been discussing something related to the torturous emotional agony with which I was living as I battled depression. What I remember clearly is that he'd emailed me these words, "Jesus came to heal shame." Shame, of course, is that evil whisper that says, in all sorts of ways, "There's something wrong with you. You're not quite right as you are."

I was no more willing to swallow that warm-fuzzy bunch of baloney than I had been prepared to believe it when Deacon Jim flaunted it around, spewing his magic, shame-dissolving potion on everyone. I was not at all convinced that Jesus had come to heal shame. In fact, if some neighbor I didn't really respect had said that heretical-sounding thing, I could have—and would have—written her off as a syncretistic, New Age whack job. Every six-year-old who has ever attended Vacation Bible School knows that Jesus came to forgive our sins, not to heal shame. That's what expensive therapists are for. End of story.

Until that moment, I'd always known my brother to be mostly of sound mind and doctrine. This is why I had to go through the motions of wrestling with that bizarro claim. Could it really be true that Jesus did come to heal shame? Could it be that when we're accepted by God in baptism, when we die and rise with Christ, we are actually made entirely acceptable? I always sort of understood that we were accepted spiritually, but I didn't think that the warranty included halitosis and wrinkles and cellulite. A claim like that is just crazy talk.

The more I thought about it, though, the more I was willing to entertain the possibility that Scott, and Deacon Jim, might just be right.

DECEIVER

As I listened to Scripture, I started to recognize the deceiver's hiss o' shame. It was that same old voice, again, that lied to Eve in the Garden, suggesting that God didn't really have her back. Remember, the one that tried to entice Jesus during his wilderness temptation? It probably sounded something like this: "You can't seriously think that you're God's son, can you? You can't really believe that God is for you? I'm going to give you the same advice I gave Eve. You should just take things into your own hands—turn this stone to bread, get yourself together, use some deodorant, suck on a breath strip. Only fools depend on what God provides."

That guy would have been fantastic in advertising, I think.

Jesus' curt reply was basically, "No thanks. I'll depend on what God provides."

I don't at all mean to suggest that Jesus is like that foolish guy in rising flood waters who waves away rescue boats and Red Cross helicopters while he waits on a roof for God to save him. I'm not even suggesting that Jesus wouldn't accept the polite offer of a breath strip today. Rather, depending on what God provides is, ultimately, about receiving the truth that we are worthy simply because God says we are. There are so many voices out there hissing in our ears that, with the right product, we could be just a little better, fresher, thinner, darker, lighter, shinier, happier. Sales figures show that we have bought the lie, women. We've bought into the lie that there's something inherently wrong, bad, in need of fixing, about who we are. Those voices are everywhere.

When I listen to Jesus, though, I don't hear it. I just don't. Instead, what I hear Jesus saying to sinners like me is that, through him, we're altogether acceptable.

I hate it when my big brother is right.

And love it.

16
LOVE

Christian Bumper Fish

Zoë and I enter a large festive room, filled with pink and red balloons, that is just starting to fill up with fabulously dressed toddlers, girls, mothers and grandmothers. Zoë quickly spots her grandmother and runs toward her.

Every year my mother-in-law invites my daughter and me to a Mother-Daughter Valentine Banquet at her church. The moment Zoë and I step out of our grimy minivan and walk toward the building, I become keenly aware that the appearance bar for the evening has been set pretty high. It's simply impossible *not* to notice how incredibly beautiful and thin and tan and polished and well-coiffed and ironed the women are, and how unmussed and well-dressed the girls are. I don't hold it against them; I'm just noticing.

As a lover of color and design, it's the outfits on the little girls that really wow me. I never even realized I shopped "off the rack" until my first Valentine Banquet with Grandma. Honestly, I'd never even *seen* dresses like these before. Almost every girl wore a dress that was neatly tailored, with rich gorgeous fabrics, matching hair bows, coordinated tights and shiny shoes. Each appeared to be one of a kind, with the lone impressive exception of those that had been custom-stitched in two or three various *sizes* so that the outfits of sisters and mothers would match.

Each year, for the twelve weeks preceding the banquet, I go through some exhausting moral gymnastics deciding what Zoë and I will wear for the gala. Because there are plenty of days during the year when I'm not even able to identify what clothes I've actually *worn* during the day until I take them off at bedtime, the annual winter fashion dilemma is more than a little ironic.

In November, pawing through the racks, I was torn, because I really wanted Zoë to wear a great dress—as great as they come for under twenty bucks. I started saying things to myself like, *If I got this sparkly red dress now, four sizes too big, she could wear it for Christmas Eve, the Valentine Banquet, and then the next Christmas Eve and then the* next *Valentine Banquet.* And then it struck me that I could maybe even squeeze another year or two out of the dress, since by then she would be a preteen and would want to wear inappropriate, sexy, skin-tight clothes. This is what I do, with the moral gymnastics. Truly, I'm an Olympic medalist with this stuff. Ultimately, I couldn't justify purchasing a novelty dress, but it certainly was not for lack of trying.

I decided the closest we could get to formal would be to go with classic black and white. I have a long black dress with some white flowers and Zoë has some sort of a groovy, swirly, black and white print dress. I happened to mention to Zoë, offhandedly, that it was a bummer we didn't have anything more festive. What I was picturing in my mind was she and I in matching, custom-made, red velvet dresses, each with a pink satin heart embroidered in the center, and maybe red- and pink-striped tights. And sparkly red ruby slippers like Dorothy wore in *The Wizard of Oz*.

While I had been imagining Dorothy, Zoë was picturing something a little more like the Tin Man. Always one for festive fashion, she went right to work, whipping us both up some flashy accessories. Apparently she'd found a yard or two of shiny silver costume fabric, the kind an ice skater might wear if she was skate-miming a wad of tin foil. Or the Tin Man. Before I knew it, Zoë had crafted, for both of us, matching silver belts, head bands and scarves. Zoë had even tied a strip around her neck like a choker necklace. When she offered to make me a choker, I politely passed.

Now I was really in a propriety pickle. Choosing not to buy a brand-new dress for the event was one thing. Having the nerve to show up in something that wasn't even red or pink seemed like pushing the envelope. But now we were going to arrive as heavily tinseled, black and white Christmas trees.

Unaware of our clownishness, Zoë was electric with delight. What girl doesn't like to shine a little? Eventually I decided that I would wear my human tinsel out of love for that girl. If we got there and she realized that we were indeed the spectacles I feared we might be, we could always lose the accessories and go back to black and white. No harm, no foul.

I felt more than a little anxious as we entered the decorated gym. Wide-eyed, Grandma grinned, "Well, don't *you two* look special." I've never been so thankful that my mother-in-law is not overly concerned with appearances. Grateful that I didn't know anyone else at the church, I just tried not to make eye contact with any of the other guests.

Never once during the evening did Zoë show any doubt that she was any less princess-like than the girls in the $175 dresses. Taking my cues from her, I tried to relax into my tinsel, silently chanting the soothing mantra, *It's what's on the inside that counts. It's what's on the inside that counts . . .*

APPEARANCES

For a lot of us, the words that were drummed into our heads, as average-looking little children, were, "It's not what's on the outside that counts. It's what's on the *inside*." If our caregivers were worth their salt, anyway, they taught us that looks aren't everything. And yet when we heard them say those two words, that looks "aren't *everything*," we knew, intuitively, that, if not everything, they were at least *something*.

Whether we like it or not, appearances do give others information about who we are. Before a new acquaintance digs below the surface to find out if we're kind or spiteful or generous or dishonest or genuine, she will already have noticed if we're wearing tinsel, if we're a decorated officer in uniform, if we're a tattooed skinhead, if we're dark-skinned or light-skinned, if we're an on-duty medical professional, if we're very tall, if we use a wheelchair or if we're a convicted felon marked by a bright orange jumper. The length of our fingernails, the limp of our gait and the labels on our clothing all give a new friend visual clues about who we are. Sometimes those clues tell the truth about who we are. Often, they cloak our truest identity.

If our new friend is visually impaired, those of us who would hide behind our fabulous clothes are simply out of luck. The auditory and kinesthetic clues we *cannot* hide—our attention to others, a quick temper, our nervous anxiety, a critical tone—will most certainly trump the fantastic outfit we've chosen that so easily fools the sighted.

Though a sighted person can *collect* visual data, possibly while people-watching at the bus stop, she won't necessarily know how to interpret what she sees. She won't know if the woman wearing simple clothing is financially poor, with few fashion choices, or whether she is someone, once rich, who has chosen to embrace poverty as a way to stand in solidarity with those in want. A people-watcher at the bus stop won't know if the thin woman rushing to work has a naturally rapid metabolism, or whether she's in the deliberate process of starving herself to death. The casual observer won't know whether the woman with a bruised face is a risk-taking snowboarder, or whether, against her will, she lives in constant risk within the walls of her own home. Visual indicators may or may not tell others the truth about who we are. This, of course, is also true for tailored red velvet dresses. In my sane moments, I realize this.

What these markers mean to each of us, personally, is a different story entirely. Some of the markers that identify us have been chosen for us—our complexions and curls and bones and height and the scars we did not choose. Other marks we have chosen to bear: the hues of our makeup, the placement of our piercings, the self-inflicted cuts, the tightness or looseness of our T-shirts and—assuming it's not a bad hair day—the style of our hair. Some of these symbols, both those chosen and unchosen, are ones around which we've constructed our entire identities.

We've been taught that looks aren't *everything*. Of course they aren't.

But they are *something*.

BELONGING

Some of the marks we bear identify us as belonging to someone else. A velvety tailored dress that matches Mommy's marks us as belonging. Engagement rings, and in certain cultures nose rings, mark someone—usually a woman—as belonging to another. Amish men stop shaving after marriage to mark themselves as belonging to another. Wedding rings most certainly signify belonging to another—so much so that clever, deceptive spouses will purposefully remove and pocket them—or *purse* them—on the way into a bar.

We are also marked as belonging to groups. A sorority T-shirt, a ring with an indented family crest, a baseball uniform, Scout badges and lodge beanies are marks of inclusion and belonging.

The very facial features by which we're recognized as unique can also mark us as belonging to a group. The slant of our eyes, the breadth of our noses, the fullness of our lips, the kink or curl of our hair, its color: all these things mark us as belonging to a particular people group.

Some of us have been marked as belonging to God. Momentarily dripping baptismal bodies, Lenten forehead ashes, modest Muslim hijabs and Jewish circumcised penises all signal—for a moment, for a few hours, for a day, for a lifetime—that we belong to a divine Other.

Though Christians have no permanent, visible symbol of belonging, some of us like to mark ourselves anyway. We press metallic silver fish, sometimes entire schools of them, onto the backs of our SUVs. We might select a gold cross or a silver fish to wear around our necks. If we're particularly daring, we might even tattoo a wee little goldfish on our ankles.

Whether or not Christians needed to be marked, visually, as belonging to Jesus, was a hot issue in the early church. As sisters and brothers learned how to live together as Jews and Gentiles in one family, a Jewish faction in Philippi insisted that Gentile Christians—the men anyway—needed to undergo ritual circumcision to mark their belonging in the family of faith.

Writing from prison, the apostle Paul, who had established the church there, was absolutely unglued about this situation. He was much more alarmed about Christians being required to bear a physical mark of belonging than he was about chains or guards or bars or prison food. In his letter to the Philippians, Paul vehemently rejects these circumcisers, whom he calls "mutilators of the flesh" (Philippians 3:2). There is no extra sign, Paul insists, outside of faith in Jesus Christ, which marks Christians as belonging.

I don't think we can be too hard on those misguided guys, because we still sort of like to do this. Though we're not necessarily cutting off any skin flaps, many of us really have grown quite attached to the stylized fish symbol. Justifying ourselves, we repeat the story we've heard about early persecuted Christians. When he or she met someone along the road, a follower of Jesus would trace a covert arc in the dirt of the ground. If the other person was also a Christian, he or she would trace a mirroring arc, making the sign of the fish. Safety confirmed and fellowship established, the wind would blow, a rain would come, and the fish would return to dust.

So it's sort of funny that that's how those of us who live in a homeland where we're not being persecuted have come to stick and decorate and mark ourselves in bold public declaration that we belong to Jesus.

The fact is, after the baptismal waters have dried and Eucharist crumbs have been brushed away, there are no designated physical signs that mark an individual as belonging to Jesus Christ.

RECOGNIZABLE

I'm not saying that people won't look at us and know that we belong to Jesus. Jesus specifically *did* want everyone to know we were his. At the end of his ministry he even gave particular instructions about how his followers were to be marked. "A new command I give you: Love one another. As I have loved you, so you must love one another. By this all men will know that you are my disciples, if you love one another" (John 13:34-35).

When people looked at Christians, they were supposed to recognize a follower's belonging to Jesus by her love for others. She was supposed to *look* something like Jesus. After all, even if they aren't *everything*, looks *are* something.

And though no historical sources suggest that any Christ-followers in the first century were tattooing their ankles or sticking twig fish to their donkey's backsides, I suspect Paul would have been concerned about any ritual or mark that would have been required for inclusion in the family. Paul knew what I too often forget: that there's something more real, more true, than what meets the eye.

I confess that too often I'm tempted to judge folks by their appearances. Instead of furrowing my brow because of a woman's electric green hair, pierced lip or tattooed forearm, however, my own personal, signature brand of sin is to judge the ones who look makeover fantastic. This is my unchecked sinful impulse.

When I'm thinking clearly, though, I realize that the CEO who is all put together every day might put less *time* into her attractive appearance than the woman, like me, who is meticulously combing every thrift store in town for just the right accessory to coordinate with her ratty old orange denim jacket. I can fathom that the one whose face routinely looks so Cover Girl fabulous might possibly spend less *energy* on her appearance than someone, like me, who has got to coordinate the socks with the hair clips with the belt buckle. The one whose cute heels make my feet ache when I see her most likely spent less *money* on those stylish shoes than someone, like me, who has paid too much money for purple patent leather Doc Marten boots so that I don't look like someone who would wear cute taupe heels.

When I'm in my right mind, I realize that appearing attractive, by whatever standard, isn't sinful. Where we get off track in this obsession with appearance is in the way we spend the time, energy and resources we've been given. Wherever we pour that stuff, says Jesus, is where our heart is. We're on the right track, though, when we attempt to faithfully reappropriate the *excess* time, energy and money we pour into our appearances, whether we look Cover Girl fantastic, polka-dot funky or pseudo-carefree grunge.

Naturally pale skin that is beautifully bronzed or chocolatey skin that melts into a deeper shade of mocha in the sunshine: these are examples of why I can't judge people by their appearance the way I'd secretly like to. One woman's skin darkens because she's been weeding an elderly neighbor's garden. Another's hue changes because she's been river-rafting with friends who need extra physical assistance. Another woman, naturally lighter-skinned, garners beautifully bronzed skin because she has meticulously scheduled a series of time-consuming appointments and paid money so she can lie alone in a hot, sweaty tanning booth. This is why it's just not as easy to judge people by their appearances as I wish it were. For this reason, when I'm in my right mind, I try to give each one the benefit of the doubt.

Monitoring the appearance of others—not to mention wasting too much time, energy and money on my own—is simply one example where I find myself dealing in a currency entirely unrelated to the one with which God seems to be working.

Clever Ways We Like to Candy-Coat Our Own Personal Sinfulness

1. *When carefree college students drink to excess, we call it drunkenness. When we do it, we're celebrating.*

2. *If our mothers routinely buy more than they need because it's on sale, we call it greedy hoarding. When we do it, it's smart shopping.*

3. *If other guests eat to excess at a wedding reception, we secretly suspect they're gluttons. When we do it, we are enjoying God's good gifts. Obviously.*

4. *If a neighbor neglects the necessary work of maintaining her kitchen or yard or home, it's lazy slothfulness. When we do it, we're embracing sabbath.*

5. *If our gorgeous archenemy buys insanely expensive cosmetics, she's wasteful and vain. When we do it, we're making the most with what God's given us.*

6. *If a cousin devours steamy romance novels, she's committing the sin of lustfulness. When we do it, we're embracing a diverse range of literature.*

7. *If an acquaintance fails to kick her bad habit, we call it an addiction. When it's us, we call it our one enjoyment.*

8. *If someone with less money than us purchases a useless novelty item, we*

call it an irresponsible extravagance. When we do it, it's a great find.

9. If someone with more money than us enjoys an exotic vacation, it's a self-ish indulgence. When we do it, it's a needed rest.

10. If a Hindu family constructs a household shrine at the center of their home to a god that promises to satisfy, we call it idolatry. When we do it, we call it an entertainment center.

JESUS

Jesus expects his followers to be *marked* by love. Their lives will be known for generosity, impartiality, sacrifice and willful self-giving. This is not to say, though, that there might not be private marks, intimate ones, known only by Christ, representing allegiance to him and to the way of love. Jesus' own risen body was marked by scars that testified to a life of love and a death of love.

Though appearances aren't everything, they are something. Sometimes our bodies *are* marked by signs of love. Something about our appearance does symbolize Christ's love being expressed through our physical bodies. To catalog them here, though, would be to reduce them, to return to chains, to reject grace. Wary of that risk, I still want to sketch a minimal montage—just to stimulate your holy imagination—of what those private marks could look like.

The bald scalp of a woman, who has shaved her head in solidarity with a friend receiving chemo, resonates with the incarnational reality of Jesus Christ.

The tongue of an English speaker who is learning Spanish, in an attempt to love her Latino neighbors, is marked by the boundary-transcending love of Jesus Christ.

A trim body—or even a naturally thick one—who pauses from eating once she has received her daily bread, veggies, fruit, meat and dairy, might belong to a follower of Jesus.

The monotonous khaki pants wardrobe, or the handsewn one, or the jazzed-up bargain thrift-store one, could suggest a moderate use of kingdom resources on one's self, generated out of love for others.

An anxiety-free face, whether round or gaunt, can signify one who has found rest in Christ.

On another face, lip gloss and dark mascara belie the fact that an individual is fasting, privately, to the Lord.

The woman or man whose arm muscles have developed from caring for a growing infant every day is marked by love.

A small scar that is healing may mark one who has given a kidney to a neighbor in need.

When our bodies bear marks of love, they point to the kingdom reality of a people who are marked by their love for others.

Hear me: I'm not suggesting that we fall back under the law. Or even that we establish a new one that involves horribly plain clothes or an entirely accessory-free way of living. I'm just saying that, as those who belong to Jesus, we're meant to be *marked* by love.

Even though we like to say that love is mostly invisible to the naked eye, Jesus had the odd notion that others would see it, notice it and recognize that we're his.

17

TOUCH

"Burrito Me!"

Each moment, millions of receptors sensitive to caresses, pokes, burns, hugs, abrasions, massages and butterfly kisses function to ensure human survival. The information we receive through our skin—when we touch a hot stove or grab the blade of a knife—sends signals to our brains that alert us to danger. These same receptors also allow us to experience pleasure. It turns out that the pleasure part, especially the sexual kind that so often leads to the birth of babies, goes a long way toward ensuring the survival of the species as well. The capacity to experience and respond to physical touch is the way we've been made.

When those receptors aren't functioning, trouble eventually ensues. When people are affected with the disease of leprosy, which Jesus encountered in his ministry among the sick, the message signaling the pain that wounds or burns or abrasions would typically send to the brain is interrupted. Though this might sound like a fantastic affliction if you've just burned your neck with a curling iron or nail-gunned your hand to the floor, it's really not all it's cracked up to be. Lepers' lives are often in danger precisely because bodily pain does not alert them that something is wrong. Not only this, but Jewish ritual law excluded those living with leprosy from experiencing the pleasant kind of touch by others who were considered ritually "clean," even though they couldn't feel it anyway. Talk about a double whammy.

In Jesus' touching and healing of lepers, he restored them to health as people who could avoid dangerous or life-threatening touch while enjoying safe, pleasant touch from others. In doing so, Jesus affirmed that these bodies were *created* to experience both pleasure and pain.

It's the design.

ALL AGES

I have always felt certain that this need for touch is why human beings don't spring out of the womb full-size. As someone who has given birth, I realize there are other practical reasons, but I think this is a big one. I learned from a friend who's an occupational therapist that when we were in the womb, we felt the comforting pressure of uterine walls defining our edges. Pressed through a narrow passage, we were finally squirted out, untethered, into a terrifying sea of freedom. Ideally, we were then pressed against our mother's warm body, held to her breasts and embraced by our father's strong arms. Once again, now outside the womb, we're made to experience safety, affirmation, nurture. Football-sized, we could easily be strapped to a front, slung on a back or scooped up into an arm for easy transport. The wonder of the small, portable design is how it invites nurturing touch.

As an infant, my daughter Zoë loved to be tightly swaddled in a receiving blanket. Though my beloved grandmother found this altogether disturbing and insisted that I was torturing her great-granddaughter, I continued to swaddle. I understood where my grandmother was coming from. Though I, personally, wouldn't want my arms bound to my side either, I knew my girl had no idea yet what to do with hers. It became obvious that not having to deal with them actually came as a pretty big relief to Zoë. To prove it, I videotaped my baby lying in her crib, tightly bound, with the most satisfied little baby smile you'd ever want to see. She was in baby heaven. To this day, she and my sons will occasionally hand me their big-kid-sized blankets at bedtime and, begging me to wrap and squeeze, shout: "Burrito me, burrito me!"

We were made to experience the bodily sensations of touch.

TOUCHABILITY

Without a doubt, children are meant to receive warm nurture from their parents. A number of years ago, in an email, a childhood friend of mine wrote me, "My children usually have wet hair because I kiss the tops of their heads so much." Gross, right? Although I thought it was weird, the idea sort of started to grow on me and I started doing that moist thing too. I'm eight years in and I haven't stopped.

When the first one toddles downstairs in the morning to greet me, usually one of my boys, often still wrapped in a blankie like a loose, soft-shell tortilla, I just can't help but squeeze him and run my hands all over him. Since I'm no longer changing diapers or giving baths or dressing them anymore—which I'm not complaining about—that morning caress might be one of my only shots during the day to give him the kind of touch for which he was made. I cup his smooth face in my hands. I kiss his sweet cheeks and the top of his sleepy head. I run my hands down his back. I envelop him in a big squishy embrace. Each one of my children is so fabulously yummy I absolutely hate the thought that one day I'll have to stop this.

This said, I don't think that extending physical affection to children, and receiving it for that matter, is supposed to be the sole propriety of mommies. The year after I graduated from college, my roommate gave birth to a precious son. If his mama was asleep in the mornings, I'd occasionally strap him to my chest and take a walk or run to the nearby grocery store. Thinking back on it now, I don't want to believe that I made that trip on roller skates, but I can't be certain. In the absence of any sort of dating life that year that might have involved some nice touching, I remember being keenly aware that the good gift of holding that boy actually met some of my natural human longings for touch. Not all of them, but a lot of them. The fact that it happened to be very satisfying for me *and* for him is part of one genius plan for children to receive nurture.

NOT JUST KIDS

And though children's need for touch can be met in a wide range of socially acceptable ways, things gets a little dicier in adulthood. Holding the hand of a child you do not know at church as you lead her to the music room, or tousling her hair, is probably pretty acceptable. Try doing that to her father and you've opened up a whole other inappropriate can of worms.

Though our oversexualized culture celebrates all kinds of sexual touch outside of marriage, and grudgingly tolerates sexual touch within marriage, there aren't a lot of other models for single adults, or married ones experiencing loneliness, to get natural touch needs met. I'm thinking in particular about the older adults who languish at home or in nursing homes. I'm thinking of women and men in painfully lonely, distant marriages. I'm thinking of some of my single friends who live alone, without cuddly, friendly pets. I'm actually thinking of many of the people I know. A lot of us aren't receiving the nurturing touch for which we've been made. This causes me to wonder if maybe we can't get a little more creative about it, and generous, than we have been up to this point.

Welcome touch, whether shoulder to shoulder, hand to hand, face to face, or belly to belly, puts us into relationship with others. An infant experiences, in a warm embrace, that she is worth receiving. A child learns, as he's carried to bed, that he is cherished. A friend is reminded, by a tender hug, that she is not alone. A lover is assured, in private intimacy, that he is desired. A grandparent is assured, by a gentle massage, that she is not forgotten. Through touch, these bodies have been designed to give and receive love.

DAVID

When my stepfather was hospitalized recently, I visited him with my mom. Entering his hospital room, my mom dropped all her things on a chair and moved right to his side. Holding his hand, she greeted him. Feeling his warm forehead, she quickly wet a washcloth to create a cool compress and placed it gently across his brow. Asking if he was thirsty, she reached for a cup of ice and slowly, gently spooned small cubes onto his tongue.

As I had been the beneficiary of the same gentle nurture when I'd been sick as a child, I shouldn't have been surprised. Still, I was moved by the attentive physical care that she offered him.

Though he was suffering, he was so grateful for that cool cloth that my mom kept replacing every few minutes. In light of all the torturous tests and treatments he'd been receiving for days on end, he turned to me and confirmed of her tender touch, "That's the best thing going."

And I know it was.

18

RELATIONSHIP

The Truth About Bodies
You Won't Hear on MTV

Recently I came across a picture of an old friend online. It looked as if Carrie had lost some extra weight. Actually, a *lot* of extra weight. It was a small thumbnail image, though, so I couldn't really tell for sure. I'm a bit of a graphic artist, and I can tell you that if a webmaster isn't on top of these things, web graphics can get smooshed completely out of shape. Maybe Carrie had just been stretched. For the sixteen years I'd known her, though, she'd always been heavy. So I was a little curious.

I confess that I'm never really sure how to handle these situations. I didn't want to email my friend to say that she looked absolutely *great*, especially if she'd just been digitally stretched. I was also terrified of reinforcing the culture's sinister insistence that appearing svelte even *matters*. On the other hand, I have always appreciated the gracious noticing of confident women who have blessed me with their affirming words about my body. But then, back to the first hand, I'm always afraid I'll tell someone who's lost weight that she looks super-duper and then find out she's been suffering from some horrible disease. And on it goes. I'm really a mess with these things.

Thankfully, when I finally ran into Carrie in person recently, a family member was with me. Genuine, and far less tangled up with these debilitating thoughts than I, she simply burst out, "Wow, you look fantastic! What *happened?!*" Carrie, who I suspect must surely hear this a lot these days, seemed absolutely fine with the outburst and all the gawking. We invited Carrie to join us for dinner the next evening and the story came tumbling out. Well maybe it didn't *tumble*, exactly, but we did needle her until she gave us the whole scoop.

About eighteen months earlier, Carrie explained, her sister Jean had expressed concern about Carrie's weight. Though I suppose that's what families do, I'd never before known the "concerned intervention" to be very effective when it comes to weight loss. Oh sure, every once in a while it might work on a celebrity drug addict reality show, because that's some good TV. In the real world, though, most of us who already know we're fat aren't usually transformed just because our mothers or sisters place the living room furniture in an intimate circle and gather more loved ones to *tell* us we're fat.

The scene Carrie described, though, had a compelling edge. Carrie and Jean's father had died, too young, of heart failure. This, of course, increased Jean's concern for her sister. Here's where it gets good. Jean specifically wanted the assurance that Carrie would be healthy enough to care for her children, Carrie's niece and nephew, if anything should ever happen to her.

Isn't that something? Not the sister part, but the *Carrie* part. Moved by her love for her family, she decided to manage her body weight so that she would be healthy and strong enough to love them well. Though she did end up looking good, by the world's dumb old standards, what actually *drove* her was love of another.

I thought that was just fabulous. In fact, as I listened, I decided that this was the best story I'd heard in months and that I was going to tell it to everyone I knew. And maybe write a book. I was blown away that Carrie had been moved, compelled, transformed to do a hard thing—something she had not done, already, out of care for herself—out of love for her family. She expressed her fidelity to others with her body.

Because bodies have been made for relationship, how perfectly *right* is that?

OBEDIENCE TO THE LAW

Not all of us have really grasped that big idea that we were made to be in relationship with God and others with our bodies. In fact, those of us who fancy ourselves to be quite sophisticated sometimes enjoy noticing how primitive, and possibly a little ridiculous, God's earliest bodily commandments were. "If men who are fighting hit a pregnant woman and she gives birth prematurely but there is no serious injury, the offender must be fined whatever the woman's husband demands and the court allows" (Exodus 21:22). I mean, seriously, how often does that even happen? Or, "Anyone who has sexual relations with an animal must be put to death" (Exodus 22:19). I don't think I really want to know how often that one happens. Or, "If you come across your enemy's ox or donkey wandering off, be sure to take it back to him" (Exodus 23:4). Does that really have to be said?

The ancient Israelites understood, though—in a way that many of us cerebral, sophisticated moderns do not—that fidelity to God and love for others is expressed through our bodies.

They got it.

Then when Jesus showed up on the scene, he fulfilled, in his body, the entirety of God's law. As might be expected, this was more than a little disconcerting for many faithful Jews who had, for generations, expressed their faithfulness to God by strict obedience to the laws that God had established. Even the Jews who *responded* to Jesus, who embraced the in-breaking kingdom, had some sorting out to do about which parts of the law should be scrapped and which ones continued to remain authoritative. Understandably, it was all pretty confusing.

A lot of Christians today, though, get just thrilled about being released from the regulations of the law. We absolutely love it. We rejoice that, in his fulfillment of it, Jesus did away with the law's binding constraints. While this is certainly *true*, were we ever under it? Did we diligently apply ourselves to keeping the law and, when we broke it, make restitution before God by sacrificing pigeons and goats and lambs and squirrels?

I didn't.

And yet many of us, overly zealous, have thrown out the Old Testament regulations, kit and caboodle, like stinky melon-rind, banana-peel, coffee-grounds trash that probably should have been picked through first and added to the compost pile.

REINTERPRETATION

Jesus was a bit more sensitive this way. He was a little more discerning with which laws could be chucked out with the trash and the many more that would become the rich soil for new life when rightly understood, through him. To the consternation of so many diligent rule-keepers, he reinterpreted the law by turning it on its head when, on the sabbath, he healed, picked grain and gave life. Though these all sound pretty mundane to us now, each one was actually pretty radical back in the day.

Though he reinterpreted the law, Jesus did not throw out the banana peels with the un-recyclables. Instead, Jesus assumed—in a way many of us today do not—that his followers would continue the kinds of holy bodily practices that knit their hearts to God's. This is nowhere more clear than in Matthew's Gospel. Jesus said, point-blank, that he was the fulfillment of the law. Since no one understood what that meant, he explained it in his Sermon on the Mount. With words he painted for his listeners a picture of what fulfillment of the law, in him, looked like.

You know not to murder with your hands, he explained, but don't murder with your tongue. You know not to commit adultery with your body, but don't do it in your mind. You know not to break oaths you've made before heaven and earth, but don't make them at all—just be a person of your word. You know that the law says to love your neighbor and hate your enemy, but instead, love your enemy. In his person, Jesus ushered in a new law of love.

Because Jesus probably had a hunch we'd try to throw out the reusable organic garbage with the regular trash, he continued on in his introductory lecture in Law 2.0 by redefining the old practices that actually do serve to bind our hearts to God's.

Assuming that his followers will continue to practice the giving of alms by giving to the needy, he teaches them to do it without fanfare. Assuming that his followers will continue to pray, he stipulates that they do it in secret. Assuming that his followers will continue to fast, he teaches them to do it cheerfully, and possibly with a little blush and mascara for good measure. Assuming that they will honor the sabbath, he guides them into a life-giving celebration of God's gift of sabbath rest.

Though some of the law did get thrown out with the trash, Jesus placed a lot of it on the compost pile; there, it became the fertile soil for a whole new way of living.

Specifically, Jesus assumed that his followers would still use their hands to give to the needy. They'd still be on their knees in prayer. They'd still keep their mouths shut, fasting, to align their hearts with God's. They'd refrain from working with their bodies on the sabbath.

Jesus assumed that fidelity to God, and love for others, was expressed bodily.

Stuff It Sort of Seems Like Bodies Were Made to Do

1. *Work*

2. *Bless*

3. *Serve*

4. *Create*

5. *Build*

6. *Love*

7. *Pray*

8. *Play*

9. *Worship*

10. *Procreate*

UNITED WITH GOD

Today I was walking with a friend who humbly shared a story about eleven chocolate-free years. As you might imagine, I gobbled that story up like a yummy snack-size bag of M&M's. Sachko had sort of stumbled into chocolate-free living when a friend asked her to join her for thirty days of abstaining from ... anything. For whatever reason, on that day chocolate seemed like the obvious choice. When the thirty days were up, Sachko just kept going.

At its worst, Sachko explained, the practice left well-meaning friends bumbling apologies for accidentally serving some chocolatey treat. At its best, though, the discipline would quietly turn Sachko's face toward God each time she breathed an unnoticed "No thanks." Each chocolatey treat avoided reminded her to trust in what God provides.

That inspiring tale almost made me want to forsake chocolate. But not quite.

During this period, in preparation for Sachko's wedding, decisions about cake flavor had fallen to her fiancé. Having purposed to offer guests—and bride—a *choice* among flavors, he'd thoughtfully decided that various layers of the wedding cake would be different flavors. But he forgot to specify which flavor should go under the fancy ivory frosting on that very *top* layer that the bride and groom feed to each another—whether in a satisfying, smearing way or a polite, sickeningly sweet way—while hundreds of eyes watch their every move.

As the first slice was being cut, the newlyweds realized the cake had been crowned with chocolate. Silent, they looked at each other wide-eyed. To all the others looking on, the familiar cake-feeding ritual appeared to be an intimate moment between husband and wife. In a lightning quick flash of recognition, though, Sachko realized that there were, in fact, *three* present. Over all the chocolate-free years, Sachko had grown keenly aware of God's nearness during holy chocolate moments like that one. God's intimate nearness had been revealed, to both bride and groom, in a decidedly personal way during the sacred moment of celebration. And how right is that?

The One with whom Sachko had quietly been walking in covenant relationship for years had been recognized, known and honored. Which is sort of the whole big point. Welcoming the holy surprise of God's familiar presence in the moment, embracing an extravagant love for her and for her beloved, she ate the cake.

A lot of us in the Christian community are pretty big on the importance of having a *relationship* with God. Though that ephemeral reality can sometimes feel hard to grasp, just out of reach on some high spiritual shelf, it's actually something in which we participate with our bodies.

SINS OF THE BODY
The most obvious place where the embodied life inextricably joins

one person to another is the physical union between a husband and a wife. Many of us *claim* to believe this. Specifically, we describe the use of our private body parts—using them or not using them in relationship to other people—as a way to be faithful to God. If we keep our bodies pure before marriage, we believe, by not sharing them willy-nilly, we honor God. When a conservative Christian sexual ethic is at its best, it's being propelled by this logic. We express our fidelity to God and others by what we do, and refrain from doing, with our bodies. We avoid certain practices, save other ones for marriage and then try not to do them with other people outside of that marriage—even in our minds when the people are just in magazines or online. That's the vision.

Some of us get ourselves into trouble, though, when we parade around with hateful signs telling other people what not to do with *their* bodies, how God hates people who do those things and how those people will burn in hell for doing them. This sort of behavior becomes especially distasteful to others when it comes out that the most vocal and preachy among us have been doing all that stuff in private. That sort of public debacle really takes the edge off a good hate placard.

For whatever reason, we're much more interested in what other people are doing with their *private* parts than we are in wondering where their wallet-hands are throwing money, why their arms are hitting loved ones or how their feet are trampling others to get a bargain at the Stuffmart on the day after Thanksgiving.

The biblical witness gives much more weight—if we're simply counting the number of things God has to say about stuff—to God's heart for justice, in the public sphere, than it gives to sexual practice in the private sphere. If we're going to get all whipped up about what individuals are choosing to do with their body parts, let's please not overlook God's passionate heart for his embodied people to treat the bodies of the weak and oppressed with justice.

We express our fidelity to God and others in what we do with our bodies privately, in what we do with them publicly, and in the ways that we honor or dishonor the bodies of others.

RELATIONSHIPS

This thing about bodies being meant for relationship is an insight I seem to need to arrive at over and over again. There are some body lessons you learn once and never have to learn again. Jumping off a skateboard while clutching a rope tied to a speeding ten-speed bike—without actually releasing one's death-grip from the rope—is among these. Trust me, it only takes once.

The relationship lesson, though, keeps cycling around time and time again for me. I'm not stupid—just human.

My family is on vacation and I'm lying in bed, sicker than a dog. There is something painful brewing inside me that is going to come out; I simply cannot predict from which end the expulsion will explode. Prepared, I'm a short dash from the bathroom and I've got a puke bucket in arm's reach. I'm actually grateful that this horrible disaster has happened while our family is on vacation. I know that's a weird thing to say, but I'm relieved that my husband can occasionally stop in, give me a pitiful look, and then go to the beach or out for an ice cream treat with our three kids. By the time they've come back with sandy, sticky faces, I've once again remembered the lesson I'd forgotten since the last time I'd been sick as a dog.

What's sinister about the flu—in addition to the discomfort and despair—is that it affects a person's relationship with others. To some degree or another, this is what's devilish about all kinds of bodily limits. Injury, disease, disability, chronic pain, amputation, infertility, obesity and ultimately death can all threaten to take us out of relationship with others. They don't all have to, but they often do. That's the problem, right there.

Of course, the reverse can also be true. Our limits can also lead to the kind of interdependence for which we were made. When the body of Christ works like it's supposed to, human limits actually draw us *into* relationship with each other. Just look at the body God used to restore relationship with himself. God chose a broken body.

So there's that.

Any way you slice it, bodies were made for relationship.

BEST CHRISTMAS EVER

I bore witness to the most beautiful use of a body, recently, when an old friend invited me out to dinner to catch up. It was a few months before Christmas. Jan told me that she wanted to do Christmas "differently." *Yeah*, I thought; *don't we all?* She didn't want it to be all about the gifts, she said, and she was really going to lay down the law with her parents. "Been there, done that," I thought wryly. I've taken some dramatic Christmas steps, but despite my best attempts, I've never—personally—been able to pull off a Christmas of which I'm entirely proud.

Assuming Jan would be in the same disappointing boat as me, I didn't even bother asking her, after the holidays, how it had gone. When Jan invited me to dinner this week, though, it sort of came up naturally.

It really went great. Jan must really have employed a serious marketing campaign in the fall, I realized, because her family actually respected her wishes for a simple holiday. For Christmas she received a few goats, a hen and a share of a well. They weren't wrapped with red bows; these were donations, made in her name. The home she owned boasted no Christmas tree, no lights, no plastic reindeer, no tinsel.

Honestly, that part of the story made me feel a little sad. But I snapped back to reality when I heard how Jan *had* celebrated.

She had knocked on her neighbor's door and sort of bumbled through the explanation she'd practiced in her mind: "Hi. I'm wondering if there's anything I can *do* for you? It's Christmas, and I want to give back something to my community."

The blank stare told Jan she might need to fill out the plan a little further.

"Can I clean your gutters? Rake your leaves? Anything?"

The mouth on the face with the blank look said, "No thanks."

"Are you sure? Anything?"

"Nope, I'm good. Thanks, though."

"All right," Jan offered, "but if you think of anything, let me know."

"Okay," the needless neighbor grudgingly agreed.

Isn't that just a sad story? If that had been me, I would have left a little embarrassed and dejected. I would have glanced away sheepishly the next time I saw that neighbor. Not Jan, though. Guess what she did?

Like a fool for Jesus, she knocked on the next door.

"Hi. It's Christmas. Is there anything I can do for you? I want to give back something to my community." She knew she'd need to flesh it out for them: "I could clean your gutters, I could rake your leaves . . ."

Blank stare.

Recognizing the familiar trajectory, Jan asked, "Do you eat? I could bake you some bread."

Hesitantly, the neighbor confessed to eating.

Jan continued with this routine all around the neighborhood. Using her most persuasive tone, she tried to talk folks into a leaf-raking or gutter-cleaning. In the end, she was invited onto a few roofs. She baked a lot of bread. She made some new friends.

"It was my best Christmas *ever*," Jan reported, glowing.

As I imagined Jan scooping nasty muck out of strangers' gutters, that most beautiful snapshot of a body in gloriously right relationship with others, I couldn't help but agree.

Jan's Christmas reminded me of the guy who asked Jesus what the *numero uno* commandment was. Jesus' double-edged answer, of course, was, "Love God. Love neighbor." If you can count, you recognize that that's really two things. I don't want to seem ungrateful for the bonus commandment, but, frankly, the two-fer doesn't give me any help whatsoever. I'd much prefer to draw a clear line between which holiday shenanigans could be attributed to Jan's love for God and which ones had been done out of love for her neighbors. No such luck. I guess if Jesus couldn't divide them up, I probably shouldn't lose any sleep over it.

Bodies were given for relationship with God and others. They just were.

19

MISSION

The Look of Unconditional
Love and Acceptance

When Peter and I were dating, we did this thing where we'd look around and notice other couples: in the mall, airports, restaurants and parades. Specifically, we'd take note of the ones who seemed absolutely tickled to be in each other's presence. We'd also notice the distracted individuals who looked like they might have been happier taking out the garbage or polishing silver or cleaning a toilet than sharing a tasty meal with their dinner partner at T.G.I. Friday's.

During this season of noticing, Peter and I coined the phrase "the Look of Unconditional Love and Acceptance." That's right: the Loulaa. It's a recognizable facial expression, just like crabby, disappointed, nonplussed or thrilled. The Loulaa is pretty much what it sounds like. When someone's gracious face meets the face of another with complete acceptance and delight, that's the Loulaa.

Try looking for the Loulaa next time you're out at a restaurant. Don't worry if you're not an experienced eavesdropper. You won't even need to know what words are, or are not, being exchanged between a couple four tables over. The facial expression, the tilt of the head, the gaze of the eyes will say it all.

I once read that there's an actual science to this kind of noticing. Apparently, educated practitioners can glance at the pictures of movie stars in the tabloids and glean insightful, crystalball sort of information about Hollywood's hottest couples. From the tilt of a head or the inattention of eyes, they can deduce which relationships are on solid ground and which ones are on sinking sand.

Technically, I suppose, the Loulaa is something you do with your face, but really it happens when a face and heart and whole body work together to express complete, unfettered acceptance of another. You'll never see it happen with a clenched fist or a disgusted hip tilt or angry crossed arms. It's just not possible.

Can you picture what this human expression, without a hint of judgment, looks like? I hope you've seen it before, but I never assume that anyone has.

Though many of us have had little tastes of the nourishing Loulaa—from a grandmother or a Sunday school teacher, a parent or a friend's mom—it's likely not been the main staple in most of our relational diets. Instead, the expressions we've more often received, the ones that reflect for us our worth, have seemed preoccupied, judging, angry, resentful, disinterested or absent. The trusted faces to whom we have turned—human, naturally self-absorbed—have not always accurately reflected for us our inestimable worth.

I say this without intending to imply judgment—even though I can hear how it sounds like that's *exactly* what I meant to imply. I might possibly have been a wee bit more judge-y before I had kids, but now I'm pretty aware that being naturally self-referenced is inherent in the human condition. Mine, anyway. And I'm not even juggling as many balls as a lot of women are managing as they care for their children and families. Broken human beings, naturally wrapped up in our own selves, and juggling way too many balls on behalf of others, don't always succeed in getting *outside* of ourselves in order to be fully present to someone else.

Though made to reflect the inherent value of others, human faces instead communicate messages like, *I'm trying to remember if today is trash day,* and *My BlackBerry is more deserving of my gaze than you are.* Without a word, our faces and the ones around us communicate, *That's an unfortunate hair situation,* and *You're not very well-read, are you?* and *I wish you were a little different than you actually are.*

A REAL LOOKER

The irony about those disappointed, distracted, disinterested glances is that they really say more about the looker than the lookee. In fact, it turns out that the Loulaa is rather *unrelated* to the actual lovability or acceptability of the person who is receiving it—especially if we agree that every individual who's been created in God's image has inherent dignity and worth.

For most of us, the irrelevance of a person's perceived value is pretty hard to swallow. In our deepest places we naturally assume that we get what we deserve. When we're found unacceptable, we're quick to believe we are. That, though, is a hissy lie of the deceiver. In truth, the Loulaa has everything to do with the person who is giving it. Even though it sounds completely dopey to say it, the Loulaa really and truly is in the eye of the beholder. Corny, but true.

When someone extending the Loulaa notices another—a child, a business woman, a foster child, a bagboy, her beloved or a non–English speaker—she sees someone who's valuable. She doesn't have to put on some fake, smiley façade of acceptance, because she actually judges the other, created in the image of God like herself, to have inherent dignity, value and worth. To her, the other is entirely precious and worth knowing. As you'd expect, this gracious noticing shows. It's evident on the face of the observer. It sort of puts a whole new spin on someone being a real *looker*, doesn't it?

Until the Loulaa, I never really understood what Jesus meant when he said "the eye is the lamp of the body" (Matthew 6:22). I'd always thought he'd been confused about that, or that there'd been a misprint. Obviously, eyes *receive* light, right? They don't *create* light. My stepfather, the ophthalmologist, will confirm this: light goes into the eyes. Light doesn't shoot out of someone's eyes unless he's an evil robot. Everyone knows this. When I started noticing the Loulaa, though, I began to understand. There's something that eyes *do* in *receiving* others as worthy and valuable and precious. Maybe this receiving even generates light. I'm no longer comfortable insisting that it doesn't.

SHE'S GOT THE LOOK
Though Peter and I saw a good bit of the look on flirty, giddy first dates, the Loulaa certainly isn't reserved for romantic situations. Please hear that. That good gift is offered to all sorts of others by grandmothers, neighbors, babies and even—I am assured by dog lovers—canines. It's that slobbery grin that accompanies the joyful "just stepped in the door after work" racing-around frenzy of mounting and pawing that goes on. With dogs. And possibly some people.

Even if you're not a dog person, you can use your imagination to picture a gracious warm face that smiles upon you, entirely delighted, for absolutely no reason at all. Without a single word, the Loulaa says, *I enjoy who you are, as you are. Don't change a thing. You're just right.*

Pretty yummy, isn't it?

Whenever a retreat leader or spiritual guide invites me to picture Jesus in my mind, this is the sort of face for which I search. I haven't actually heard Jesus saying any of those "you're totally the greatest" Up With People words. I do think, though, that his face communicated clearly the prayed and spoken and lived message that, because of each person's inherent belovedness by the Father, he was *for* them.

Start to notice the image of Jesus' face that you carry in your own mind and heart. Can you see it? Is it turned toward yours? I hope it is. We can't rule out the possibility, though, that your blurry Jesus might be scowly or furrowed or judging. I hope not, but it's actually pretty imaginable.

Though no ancient paparazzi captured the actual image, the witness of the biblical account leads me to believe that Jesus' face probably *did* look judgmental when he spoke to people who were self-made, or painfully religious, or stingy with their wealth, or who had dirty insides, or who judged others, or who hadn't known pain but had still strapped heavy loads to others' backs. I hope that's not you, but it may be.

I'm pretty certain, though, that when Jesus' face shined upon those who knew themselves to be needy—those who didn't know God, or were poor, or had dirty outsides, or were used to being judged by others, or had lost a parent or spouse or child, or were saddled with heavy burdens—the expression they saw was something like the gracious Loulaa.

This is, of course, just a guess, but I'd like for you to do me the favor of seriously considering it.

WHEN IT HAPPENS TO ME

As great as the Loulaa is, many of us frequently receive a look that is the *opposite* of unconditional love and acceptance.

A few months ago I raced toward the city's public library after dropping my kids off at school. As I approached, I could tell by the empty parking lot that the library had not yet opened. Nonetheless, there was a crowd milling out front. Folks were sitting on steps and standing around chatting. I thought it might be some special early-morning party. Maybe someone had rented out the library for their special gala the way they might live it up at a local roller rink or Chuck E. Cheese's. As folks continued to float across the street toward the building, however, I realized that these were in fact people who'd been shuffled out of the homeless shelter across the street for the day, and who were waiting in the cold fog for the library to open. There were two sheriffs' deputies in an upper parking lot to monitor the peaceful waiting.

I parked my car and hopped out to run my two books on tape over to the audio-video drop slot. On the way I had to pass through the crowd of waiting library patrons. I tried to act warm, relaxed and friendly.

Seeing the expressions on those faces, though, made me realize that I hadn't looked in the mirror before I'd left home that morning. My hair was unbrushed and I was wearing my groovy, lime-green glasses. Under my unzipped sweatshirt I wore a shirt with fat pink stripes, above pajama bottoms with tiny pink, green and white stripes. Wearing no socks, I had on one fake Croc that was pink and one that was blue. Honestly, I was so funky looking that I would have been surprised if anyone in that waiting crowd *hadn't* given me a suspicious once-over. As faces glanced in my direction, each one got a little bit of a sour expression as they took me in. Inevitably they looked down at my feet and took a step back so as not to catch whatever weirdo disease I might be carrying.

I wish I could say this was the first time I had been in this situation. But I won't lie: it happens all the time. At my nephew's birth I showed up at the hospital wearing a priestly collar and fantastic, kelly green tennis shoes. It was Saint Patrick's Day. Another time I'd gotten out of my car at an intersection to help a lady who had unexpectedly rammed her SUV into a guardrail, and I was dressed like a holiday elf. I had on red- and white-striped tights, a matching hat, flower-covered combat boots and jingle bells. Or another day I was running late and got a flat tire myself. While I was frantically trying to flag down someone who actually owned a cell phone, I remembered I was wearing a bike helmet, swim goggles, a shiny soccer shirt, skater knee and elbow pads, a life vest and a faux Olympic gold medal. (There was a perfectly good explanation for this one; the others were just good old-fashioned holiday spirit.) I suppose the upside, in the case of the roadside emergency assistance situation, is that traffic actually *did* stop.

All this is to say that I've had my share of suspicious, confused, sour looks. I'm not complaining, however; although I usually think I look fabulous, I can see how I sort of invite them. If I'm going to wear jingle bells, or don swim goggles, or paint my fingernails yellow, or shave a word in my scalp, I need to be prepared to face the consequences. I get that.

The consequences—which I'm not saying I don't deserve—can be these Looks of Unconditional Rejection. More often than flat-out rejection, though, I notice the Loclaa: the Look of *Conditional* Love and Acceptance. Without a word, these dubious glances say something like, *Although I can't quite put my finger on it, there is something that is not quite right about you. I'm not even entirely sure why I want to slowly back away from you, but I do. I'd really feel more comfortable around you if you were different than you actually are.*

BLENDING

I actually became quite used to the Loclaa as a teen. When my mother would get her feathers ruffled about my unconventional appearance, my stepfather would gently remind her, "She knows how to be appropriate when she needs to be." I always found that to be a helpful distinction. Although we all agreed I looked a little goofy on most days, he was saying that if I had been going to a funeral, or to a graduation, or been speaking in front of five hundred people, I would have worn the right thing. He was right: I would have. My mom had done all she could do by giving me the tools; in a pinch, I could pull off *appropriate* if I had to.

The years have proved my stepfather right. I do know how to blend when I need to. While working as a hospital chaplain, I had enough sense to wear skirts and blazers and tasteful footwear instead of the comfy clothes and sneakers that I desperately wanted to wear. When I'm invited to preach, I try not to choose anything that will incite worshipers to think more about my outfit than about the message. When I'm a worshiping guest in a traditionally African American congregation in my neighborhood, I put forth my very, very best effort to be as well dressed as I can be. If this comes as a surprise to any of my friends at St. John's Missionary Baptist Church, which it very well may, please know that I truly am doing the best I can with what I've got.

There's something to be said for attempting to blend in. If I go to a fancy country club, for example, people are much more likely to relax and enjoy me if I'm wearing makeup, if I've used some sort of hair sculpting product, and if I have donned neatly tailored clothes, stylish shoes and coordinated gold jewelry. I think it goes without saying that I've left the nose ring at home. When I wear that uncomfortable getup, country club people can relax and chat me up by inquiring about my alma maters, world travels and career ambitions.

The wait staff, though, doesn't give me a second glance.

And there it is. Some of us have the weird privilege of coifing ourselves so that we conform to the eyes of others. In a world that values appearances, we can *pass*. I'm not recommending it, just observing. We can dress and groom and style ourselves so that we do garner the gracious attention of country clubbers, potential employers and influential women in civic organizations.

There are others, though, *precious* others, who are less like chameleons than I can be. Many African American women know the nervous look that says, *You are other. I'm not going to get too close.* Women of various ethnicities can tell their own stories of being distanced—and even dissed—socially. Individuals who live with disabilities know the anxious glance that says, *I'm not entirely convinced I won't catch what you have.* Women and men who stand at freeway exit ramps with signs that say "Will work for food" know all too well expressions of judgment, fear, disgust and disinterest.

Faces we see every day, those of clerks serving us at the grocery store and McDonald's and Walmart, are often overlooked altogether. For hours on end they can watch cell phones and pocketbooks and fingernails receive more attentive care than their own human faces. And all too often, in our youth-obsessed culture, the follicle-pigment-challenged individuals who live under gray hair—strolling at a mall or the airport or on a college campus—might just as well be wearing a cloak of invisibility. These, and so many others, are the ones upon whom God is just dying to smile, through a human face.

THE REAL FEAT

You may be thinking to yourself, *It's not so hard to project the love and warm fuzzies to a complete stranger. Grinning at a woman who just handed me a Big Mac isn't so tough.* If you thought that, you'd be right. A passing glance isn't hard to pull off. Loving an aggravating family member, on the other hand, is a real feat. What Peter and I would learn, after a decade or so of marriage, is that the Loulaa simply can't be sustained moment by moment, day by day, year after year in an actual, real relationship. Go figure. In authentic relationships we'll routinely become steaming mad, overwhelmed, terrified or desperately sad. The Loulaa is not about lying by putting on a clown face over our real ones.

It just may be, though, that extending to someone the look of unconditional love and acceptance—the way Peter and I did do when we were dating—becomes, for another, a window to grace.

Then you get to all the fun stuff.

RELATIONAL SAVANT

One of my good friends, sixteen-year-old DeCarlo, is a Loulaa savant. He really is. When we first met, I thought maybe DeCarlo was being extrafriendly and nice to just *me*. Then we went to the mall.

Honestly, my life has never been the same since I went to the mall with DeCarlo Holmes. On the drive there, I eased to a stop at a red light. DeCarlo turned to look at the person whose car was stopped beside us and then turned back to ask me, eagerly, "Who's that?!" There was a discernible edge of excitement in his voice. Somewhat amused, I answered, "I don't know who that is." I didn't say, "We live in a metropolitan area of one million people. What on earth would give you the idea that I would be able to ID a completely random stranger who just happens to be driving on Fayetteville Road?" Although I didn't say it, you can bet I thought it.

While I prayed for the light to change quickly, DeCarlo kept looking at the driver beside him and smiling and waving. He actually started to roll down the window, in order to introduce himself, just as the light turned green. Hitting the accelerator, I breathed a sigh of relief. Friendly is great and all, but you just never know when some driver isn't going to want a smiley stranger getting all up in their business.

At the mall, we parked and started to walk toward the entrance to Sears. Raising his hand in a familiar wave, DeCarlo shouted out to some folks walking back to their own vehicle, "Hey! How are *you* doing today?" He said it with the warm tone I might have used if I'd known someone for two or three decades. They smiled, answered and kept walking. This happened a few more times, with other strangers, before I finally whispered to DeCarlo, "Do you *know* them?"

The glint of excitement returning, hopeful, he answered, "No. Do *you*?"

Nope. Still no.

At the mall we visited one of those weird gadget stores. I was investigating an elbow massager when I heard DeCarlo exclaim, "Well, *hello!*" Turning, I saw him embrace a man I did not know. I hoped that DeCarlo did know him, but of course I couldn't be sure.

This continued for hours. What I learned about DeCarlo was that there was a very, very thin line between already knowing someone intimately and meeting them for the first time. In fact, it was almost invisible. That sixteen-year-old boy knew more people in Durham, North Carolina, than I even thought possible. Even on the way home he instructed me to slow the car down at a known drug corner on my street. Feeling like I was sort of protected by a force field of joy, I did. "Hey DeCarlo," a teenage girl greeted him. "Hey girl," he shouted, "how are you doing today?!"

DeCarlo knows no strangers. The reason, though, is no mystery. DeCarlo approaches every driver, every walker, every shopper as if he or she might just possibly be a long-lost friend he hasn't seen for years. Occasionally they are. Even if they aren't, though, DeCarlo makes each person feel as if he or she is the center of the world. And really, isn't that what we all want? DeCarlo has this amazing gift of making others feel seen, known and loved. He knows exactly what faces and bodies are for.

20

IMAGE-BEARING

"Yep, You Belong Together"

Thumbing through snapshots, searching for some kindred resemblance, I scanned the photos my birth mother had sent me. At age twenty-two, I had just met her, and we had decided to exchange photographs through the mail. One of the first photos showed her in first grade, with large dark eyes and dark brown hair.

Hmmm, I worried. *Maybe there's a mistake.* My summer-blonde hair and blue eyes bore little resemblance to the dark brunette six-year-old in front of me.

A few shots later was one taken during the season I affectionately like to think of as "The Summer of Love." Standing next to my birth father, Pam has lighter hair. I recognized, in her, a familiar jaw line. From him, familiar eyes, nose, furrowed brow.

For the first time in my life I understood, in my bones, what it means to be created in someone's likeness, to bear enough resemblance for someone to squint and concede, "Oh yeah, I see it now. Yup, you belong together."

JESUS

For centuries, Israel worshiped an invisible God. And although God could not be seen, the first chapter of Genesis makes the pretty wild claim that humankind, both men and women, had been created in God's image. As you might imagine, the whole invisibility situation left a lot up to the imagination. In fact, for centuries scholars have debated what it might mean to be created in the image of God. Some claim that humankind bears God's image in our ability to reason. Others point to our moral capacity. Martin Luther King Jr. named the inherent dignity and worth of every individual as the way in which we bear God's holy imprint. No one, of course, is arguing that our actual eyes and elbows and clavicles and earlobes look anything like God's.

That would be crazy.

Even though the Jews hadn't set eyes on this invisible God, they still seemed to know a little bit about what God looked like. God had a tongue that spoke creation into existence. God had lungs that breathed life into the first man. God had eyes that were all-seeing. God had a righteous right arm. You know, stuff like that.

Although it was a pretty good God-sketch, it did leave an awful lot to the imagination.

The gist of the New Testament was that, through the person of Jesus Christ, the holy outline was filled out, colored in and given three dimensions. In Jesus, humankind finally got to take a good, hard look at that once-invisible God. That's no metaphor. I mean, they really got to see and hear and touch and smell God with bones, skin, scabs, calluses and body odor.

I realize that might have been a little jarring.

Jesus really was the spitting image of his Dad. One of my favorite conversations in Scripture, reported by John, comes toward the end of Jesus' ministry. When Jesus knows that his friends are on the unseen verge of feeling utterly lost, sadly deceived and defeated by death, he tells them, "I am the way and the truth and the life." Then he continues, "No one comes to the Father except through me. If you really knew me, you would know my Father as well. From now on, you do know him and have seen him" (John 14:6-7).

His friends racked their brains. None of them remembered meeting his heavenly Dad. Philip, understandably confused, replied, "Lord, show us the Father and that will be enough for us."

Jesus answered: "Don't you know me, Philip, even after I have been among you such a long time? Anyone who has seen me has seen the Father. How can you say, 'Show us the Father'?" (John 14:8-9).

Those guys just didn't get it. The Jesus that they could see, and hear, and touch, and smell was the *exact* representation of his Father who, heretofore, had been invisible. They had actually *seen* the Father.

The mind-blowing nature of that realization is why I do not hold it against them. It was a lot to take in.

FAMILY ALBUM

Jesus really did bear a stunning resemblance to his heavenly birth father. As it soaked in, and as his friends started to think back, I'll bet the pieces sort of fell together for them. They probably started to notice the way Jesus' physical body fleshed out what they already knew about the Father of David.

Whether a person Jesus was with was important or unimportant, in the world's eyes, didn't really seem to phase Jesus much. His eyes, resting upon a leper or a child or a woman, really noticed and saw the person God had created the other to be. His ears, tipped toward those not usually heard, really listened. If you've ever met someone with a face like this, you know that you never want to let them out of your sight or range of voice again.

Hmmm . . . so that's what it looks like to resemble the Father.

I have to believe that his face probably looked mostly like the mugs of a lot of other Middle Eastern men of the day. It probably didn't glow, like it does in Renaissance paintings, or dazzle, in the same way that one on the cover of *People* magazine might. What I suspect made it particularly attractive was a quality that can be a little slippery to name. It was a peace, which sprung from his trust in his Dad. Specifically, it was as if the *absence* of the regular anxieties about food and clothing and self had freed him to be entirely *present* to the person to whom he was speaking.

Hmmm . . . so that's what it looks like to resemble the Father.

The hands that multiplied fish and bread also enjoyed a glass of wine with friends. They healed withered hands, opened blind eyes, animated paralyzed bodies, straightened bent backs and cured leprous skin. They touched the people that no one else would touch.

Hmmm . . . so that's what it looks like to resemble the Father.

The knees bent in prayer to his Father rose to walk from city to city to share the good news of the in-breaking kingdom.

Hmmm . . . so that's what it looks like to resemble the Father.

Jesus' back stooped over to wash the feet of his friends.

With his physical body, Jesus patterned for us life which really is life. He fleshed out exactly what it means to be made in the image of God.

I know I'm being a little bit . . . well, literal . . . but I'm convinced that the image of God made flesh in Jesus is *exactly* what it looks like to resemble the Father.

What Body Parts Are Really Made For

1. *Hair: to keep body heat from escaping*

2. *Eyebrows: to show others what's inside, like anger at injustice or joyful surprise·*

3. *Eyelashes: to keep irritating little fuzzy and grainy debris out of eyes*

4. *Noses: to shelter breathing holes so rain and snow and falling leaves don't fall straight into them*

5. *Teeth: to tear and chew food, and sometimes protect one's self*

6. *Hands: to sew clothes and prepare food and make other cool stuff*

7. *Legs: to facilitate mobility*

8. *Abs: to get up off the floor from a horizontal position*

9. *Fat: for sustaining life when times are lean*

10. *Butts: for sitting around on while seeing and hearing and speaking with others*

LIFE PATTERNED AFTER JESUS

This is why I think it's a little funny that Christian women assume we can do better, with our bodies, by baking them in tanning booths, coloring them with chemicals and slimming them with diet pills. It's almost as if we weren't paying attention very well.

The woman who *does* pattern her bodily life after Jesus' life, though, offers her entire self to loving him and others. She keeps Jesus' commandments by pressing her lips together when she wants to call someone an idiot. She squints her eyes shut rather than committing lustful adultery in her heart. When someone asks to borrow something, she hands it over. She raises her face to greet someone who's *not* her brother or sister or favorite neighbor or friend. Her right hand gives alms to the poor. She washes her face and spruces up her makeup when she fasts. She sits down in the home of sinners and eats with them—party food, even! She hands a cup of cold water to someone who's thirsty. She washes stinky feet. She stops using her body to sleep with someone else's husband.

With the exception of that last one, doesn't that snapshot look a lot like Jesus?

Moving like Jesus did, in relation to others, is exactly the thing for which our bodies were made. When a doctor uses her skilled hands to apply healing ointment, she imitates Jesus' motions of using his arms, hands and fingers to smear mud on a guy's eyes to heal his blindness. When an advocate seeks justice for those bound by the sex-trafficking industry, she announces release for the oppressed the way Jesus did in his inaugural address. When an employee at a bagel bakery brings home the day's leftovers for children who are hungry, in her neighborhood or at a local shelter, she imitates the motions of Jesus' body when he fed the poor.

This said, no prestigious degree, no particular skills, no carefully honed abilities are requisite to living a life patterned after Jesus Christ. Consider that Jesus also embodied the Father's love, really showed what God was like, when he was pinned, disabled, to a cross. The invisible pattern of self-giving love is what marks individuals who are being transformed more and more into the likeness of Christ.

As our bodily life begins to imitate the life, death and resurrection of Jesus, people who know our Father look at us, maybe sort of squinting, and agree, "Yup, they belong together."

21

MOVEMENT

Some Tough Questions
About Simulated Exercise

Ma and Pa Ingalls. Nomadic African tribespeople. Chinese field workers.

When I try to imagine a lifestyle in which people actually work with their bodies to support themselves and their families, these are the cursory mental snippets with which I'm working.

I wish I were kidding.

Besides Laura Ingalls's folks, and the imaginary international hunters and gatherers, I just do not personally know many folks who work all day with their bodies. I know Iris, who works at a university and cleans up after college students. My neighbor Abura cares for children in her home. I know a few physical therapists. I don't know one person, though, who works in a factory. I don't know one person who works in a field. When I do glimpse one, on television, I usually gasp in astonishment, "Oh my gosh! Can you imagine what it would be like to *do* that all day every day?" If there's anyone around, they usually can't.

Mine is a cerebral life, as are those of many around me. Because I live one block from Duke University and mix regularly with Dukies, I know a number of people who pretty much *think* for a living. Sure, they'll write some stuff every once in awhile, but I can assure you they're not getting any cardiovascular benefits from the typing. I, myself, was trained as a ministry professional. More thinking. And some praying. A little jaw music. The occasional palm lifted high to heaven. Today, as a writer and speaker, I sit most of the day. I move my fingers.

Our bodies were made to move—to faithfully steward creation and to meet human need—and a lot of us are not moving. Hear me: I don't expect any pity for being able to sit around a whole bunch. Neither do I want to glamorize the physical labor that *is* being performed today by those being underpaid for producing my food and the junk I try not to buy. I'd just like for many of us who are privileged enough to buy books to admit that many of our bodies, made for healthy movement and function, are being underused. At the same time, many more bodies, typically the ones of those who are most vulnerable, are being overused. I just don't think it was supposed to be this way. Not with the unhealthy sitting and the exploitation of beloved bodies.

D.C.

When my husband watched the ten-part miniseries *John Adams*, based on David McCullough's book about America's second president, I'd occasionally wander into the living room from sewing clothes at the dining room table or painting something fantastic. If the scenes transpiring on the television screen did not involve tarring and feathering, wartime amputations or unsavory pox pustules, I would stay awhile.

One evening I drifted in as John and Abigail Adams were arriving in America's new capital, Washington, D.C., while it was still under construction. Everywhere the eye could see were slaves at work building our nation's new seat of government. The two Massachusetts natives, both fundamentally opposed to slavery, looked on in evident discomfort as the city meant to represent their highest aspirations for life, liberty and the pursuit of happiness was being built by slaves.

Bodies weren't made to be enslaved by grueling taskmasters— certainly not bodies busy constructing monuments to freedom and justice for all. Though the subtitles make no mention of it, I have to believe that John and Abigail were thinking what I was thinking: *It's not supposed to be this way.*

DUKE

Because I live near Duke, I pass through campus several times a week. Some days I see a lone student, female, soldiering through a brutal run. Her pale face is always unanimated and determined. She is bone thin. More often than not, she wears baggy sweat pants. A long shirt hangs down past her minimal buttocks. If her arms or legs are bare, I can't help but notice how much they resemble the frail limbs of those who suffer from malnutrition around the globe. Wanting to give her the benefit of the doubt, I entertain the fleeting possibility that she has the kind of rapid metabolism that most American women would kill for. Searching for a reason, I try to believe she's fighting her way back to life after a year of brutal chemotherapy. If I'm honest, though, I believe neither. Her face, clearly suffering, gives her away.

I imagine the young woman dressing, standing before her fulllength dorm mirror, checking every angle for unsightly bulges. I suspect that this precious one who is wasting away judges her frame, and herself, too harshly. I briefly toy with the idea of shouting out something caring loud enough to be heard above her iPod. I imagine grabbing her in a warm, soft, squishy bear hug, reminding her how precious and beautiful and beloved she is, whether deathly skinny or deathly fat. Since I'm a stranger, though, I don't.

As she fades from view, I pray that someone else does.
It isn't supposed to be this way.
Not with the injurious running and the malnutrition.

SERIOUS

Although I enjoy exercise, like walking and biking and swimming in the local quarry, I'm not one of these women who is super-*serious* about fitness. I've never been maniacally driven toward excellence. Just ask my high school basketball coach. Put me in a minivan, though, and send me to the grocery store parking lot, and I become a wild-eyed competitor for the parking space requiring the least amount of actual walking to reach the store. I come by it honestly, because my mom is a circler. More patient than I am, she'll calmly troll through aisle after aisle in the mall parking lot, confidently assuring me, "We'll just wait until someone leaves." Though I'm disgusted by the slow creeping, she's always right. Invariably, someone leaves. She scoots into their spot and is ultimately vindicated in the eyes of her crabby daughter.

I have no patience for the trolling and waiting. Nor do I intend to walk seventy whole yards from my vehicle to the store. I actually have a favorite parking spot at the grocery store I typically frequent. (These, for the record, are words I never imagined I'd say.) My great spot is almost adjacent to the grocery entrance, beside PetSmart. It just takes a few steps to get into the store and a few steps back out. Should my favorite spot be occupied—heaven forbid by a pet owner—I am forced to circle. Wistfully passing by the spaces reserved for wheelchair-accessible vehicles, I try to outsmart the system by scanning for aisles I think everyone else has overlooked. Mentally positioning a gigantic, invisible, pivoting compass at the store entrance, I calculate the distance to the nearest available spot while constantly figuring in the driving-time to walking-time ratio. It's really quite an elaborate equation.

I race into the store and zoom through my shopping, so that after I speed home, I'll have time to exercise.

It's not supposed to be this way.

The absurdity of an able-bodied person burning gasoline in order to find a great parking spot to go shopping in a strip mall is trumped only by the absurdity of doing the same thing in the parking lot of a gym. Paying for the gas in order to *not* walk very far to get into a building where one is paying to exercise, on an electric-powered sidewalk, or something else that simulates an imaginary hill: well, it has got to raise some red flags, people.

Bodies made with the innate capacity to hunt for food and till the soil and lift babies have simply got to get up out of our ergonomically sensible office swivel chairs and driver's seats to move. Since it doesn't seem like a lot of us will be slopping pigs or splitting wood or baling hay any time soon, we do have to find some healthy ways to get these bodies moving.

LATE-NIGHT TV

The *old-fashioned* fitness plan, of course, was called "Wake Up at the Crack of Dawn and Work Hard to Survive." That was my grandfather's exercise routine. Today the comfort that so many Americans enjoy is the whole reason that all of us who sit in front of computers all day need to exercise in the first place. I don't think we can be surprised that bodies designed to till, plant, harvest, gather, milk, hunt, skin, build and sew are now *wanting* for some artificial exercise.

Today we wiggle a pen to purchase a prebuilt house. We drive our minivans to the grocery store to gather goods in a well-oiled shopping cart. We ride the escalator up a flight or two at the mall to buy a new bra. It seems less than shocking that most of us are now finding ourselves in desperate need of movement.

Hear me: I have no interest in shunning every modern convenience. Regularly, weekly even, I am insanely grateful that I don't have to do the backbreaking work of bending to scrub my family's

clothes clean on a washing board. Instead I throw them in a big
magic box, squirt in some special sauce and an hour later—or
three days later if I'm not paying attention—*voilà!* Clean clothes.
Had I lived during a more housework-intensive era, I'm not certain I wouldn't have simply opted for dirty and smelly. That stinky
scenario is entirely conceivable.

Today, though, in the absence of some of the once-normal
bodily work, we pay to go to a fancy gym to use their ab-busters.
We drip gallons of salty sweat in an early morning spin class. We
rise early, click on our iPods and get a run in before work. We
write a check to meet with a personal trainer after work. There's
nothing so horribly *wrong* with those things. I don't want to knock
them, because most of us truly do *need* the exercise. (I also don't
want to knock them because a friend of mine makes a living running two gyms.) I'm all about the fitness. It is, though, a unique
modern pickle in which we find our sedentary selves.

SOMETHING BETTER

I am convinced that there is something even *better* for contempo-
rary women. There's something that's even better, for our souls
and bodies, than some of the things we're doing—and even paying to do—to our bodies in the name of fitness right now. Specifically, I'm thinking that we could do some of the work that it does
take to sustain daily living with our actual bodies.

Many of us who live within a few miles of a grocery store or
farmers' market could be walking or running or biking to pick up
some staples. We might carry home a couple of five-pound bags of
groceries in lieu of pumping the metal dumbbells for stronger tri-
ceps and biceps. We could deliver our party invitations by foot, or
even by an arm stuck out after church. For free. If we do walk a few
blocks from the car, bus or train into the office, school or home, we
could pick up trash on the way. (Hint: if we were paying a personal
trainer to make us do this motion, we'd call them *squats*.)

Can we just go ahead and name it as strange that those of us who work in two-story or four-story office buildings, hospitals and schools avoid the stairs (opting for an elevator instead) and then—between bites of Cheetos from the basement vending machine—bemoan how hard it is to find time to fit artificial exercise in before or after work?

Seriously, I could go on all day with this stuff. Don't be too impressed—the griping is pretty intuitive once you get the hang of it. When we start to use our bodies to do the actual work of survival and hospitality and service, many of us will enjoy the pleasant surprise that the personal trainer becomes less requisite.

Want strong arms to carry a baby? Carry a baby. Want cardiovascular endurance? Bike or run to the library. Want an overall body workout? Shovel or rake or mow for an elderly relative or neighbor.

Possibilities for Blessed Movement

1. *Pick apples or strawberries or wildflowers. Preferably legally.*

2. *Walk to a friend's house to leave a love note.*

3. *Walk to an enemy's house to leave a love note.*

4. *Choose the farthest parking space each time you drive to the grocery store.*

5. *Walk to the grocery store.*

6. *Walk from the first grocery store to a different store because it carries hormone-free milk.*

7. *Carry home two gallons of milk.*

8. *Help your neighbor get her groceries inside when you see her vehicle pull up.*

9. *Carry laundry up and down stairs—one item at a time.*

10. *Bike to the local farmers' market or even to the actual faraway farm.*

MISSION

There's more. I also don't see any good reason that fitness needs to be truncated from our mission to love God and others.

Oh yes, I went there.

Don't worry, though, because I'm not talking about walking the treadmill with pocket Bibles under our noses. I don't mean showing up at yoga with a "Jesus said it, I believe it, that settles it, so go to hell" T-shirt. I don't even mean reaching our target heart rate by running from door to door witnessing at minimansions. Think a little bigger.

Think a lot bigger.

More thrilling than even doing our *own* errands is using our bodies to serve others. Instead of gobbling up our cell phone minutes or Facebook bytes listening to a friend's heartache, we might take a walk together so our friend could see God's compassion in a real human face. We could spend a Saturday morning that we might have gone to the gym to lift weights by helping a new neighbor move in down the street. (Clearly, spontaneity is requisite.) We might ring the doorbell of a stressed-out mom and offer to push her infant in a stroller around the block—twenty-nine times or so.

You get the idea here, right?

The doing of the regular stuff that meets real human need, ours and others, is what bodies were made to do.

I'm simply asking you to consider doing that slightly radical, completely normal thing.

22

OTHER-CENTEREDNESS

Skating Grandma, Rap Mama and the Pigment-Deficient

Margot is wondering how to explain to her daughter why women color their hair."

That was my Facebook status. When the comments started rolling in, I knew I'd hit a nerve. Honestly, no one had ever cared more about my status. Well, men still didn't care, but women were suddenly *very* interested. A sampling from the many comments included:

"Hmmm . . . vanity? Because thirty-year-olds don't like to look eighty?"

"If the barn needs painting, you paint it! Same goes for hair!"

"I think only children should have their natural hair color.

It gets mousy, people! Cover it up!"

Some had a dash of creative flair:

> "I thought we were seeking to imitate the amazing variety of shades and hues of other critters in the kingdom: the cardinal's scarlet, the red fox, the brown bear, the sleek blond cougar, etc.: except not the gray squirrel, the silver fox and the snowy owl."

> "You can go the scientific route: 'You see dear, hair goes gray because pigment cells in the hair base at the roots of the hair stop producing melanin . . .'"

> "God gave us hair and nails to use like a canvas. We can color and modify them to suit our individual personalities. How we wear our hair is a form of self-expression."

That one in particular appealed to my creative side.

Then came the explanations:

> "I highlight my hair. I don't have a stitch, or should I say a strand, of gray, but I liked being blonde much better than brown. I like some blonde because it reminds me of how my hair used to look when I was younger. I am reminded of good feelings and remembering when I was younger and carefree. I am honoring my youth as I am aging."

I thought "honoring my youth" was pure genius. Another woman shared,

> "I had colored my hair for years, then decided to grow out the gray after I had let it go playing a wino in *Little Shop of Horrors*."

This is a distinguishing feature of winos, apparently, with which I'd previously been unfamiliar. She continued,

> "I was fine with it until my friends met my older sister, who colored her hair, and asked me if she was my baby sister.

When I started coloring again, it made me feel so much younger to not have the gray."

I am so glad I posted. Until I'd read those comments, I'd always been a little judgmental about the whole thing. I don't mean that I've had unpleasant thoughts toward particular women with unnaturally copper hair or dark roots or light gray ones poking through their scalps. I just mean that I've had a little issue with the whole billion-dollar beauty empire. That empire really gets under my skin.

As I read along, it was actually the melanin comment that got to me. Suddenly it felt more than a little sad to me that cells that had once led vibrant, satisfying lives of pigmentation simply stopped producing melanin. It felt like a little death.

I guess that's the point: that is, for some women, going gray feels a little the same way. We'd rather stay colorful than go gray. We'd rather stay young than get old. We'd rather hang on to life than lose it. Ultimately, we'd rather live than die. In his Pulitzer Prize–winning book, *The Denial of Death*, Ernest Becker identifies the ways in which this subconscious impulse to deny death's impending sting drives us in ways we'd never imagine. Although I do not believe Dr. Becker mentions any Maybelline or Revlon products by name, I can't help but think about the ways we make up our faces—to suggest smoother skin, bigger eyes, darker lips and rosier cheeks—to more closely resemble the way we looked, naturally, as infants and children.

Coincidence? I think not.

WE DO IT

As a general rule, I prefer decidedly nuanced things—like the question of whether or not women ought to color their hair—to be black and white. (Or in some cases, gray and golden blonde.) Unfortunately, they're not.

While I reviewed for my husband Peter the "why do women

color their hair" comments, he turned the tables by asking me, "Why do some women *paint their glasses?*"

It felt like one of those situations in the Bible when some hypocrite asks Jesus a perfectly good entrapping question, and Jesus has the nerve to turn the whole thing around to make it about them.

Also, Peter's question was a little pointed, I believe, because I am the only woman either of us knows who paints her glasses. So I think he meant me.

I can explain. I went to Costco and bought a pair of the fattest frames I could find. I chose a black pair with lots of surface area. Then I went home and decorated them with acrylic paint. I trimmed the entire perimeter with tiny white polka dots. Because I felt like a theater marquee the whole evening, though, I scratched off most of the dots and simply left the single row across the top. So now they're still a little jazzy but without too much humor, I believe.

The question stands. Why do women paint their glasses? Still a little put out by Peter's insightfulness—as I so often am—I got up and peeked in the bathroom mirror to check things out. Sure enough, though I'm too lazy for makeup or hairstyling, I had a lot happening, visually, around my face. I had the jazzy glasses, of course, and a shiny cubic zirconium nose ring. I had about five earrings. And ever since my hair was cut too short in the front, I'd been wearing those spring-loaded hair clips. That day they were black, with white polka dots. To match the glasses, of course.

So although I wasn't coloring my cheeks or lashes or brows or lids or follicles, it turns out that I'd done essentially the same thing with all the accessories. Though I don't have imminent plans to drop any of that fantastic bling, it does makes it harder to judge freely the way I'd like to.

We're coloring all this stuff to give the illusion, to ourselves and others, that we're not aging, and that, ultimately, we're not dying. Except that we are. Whether we're eleven and still headed toward some peak optimal attractiveness or whether we're past our prime, we're all aging, and we're all going to die.

GRANDMA

Every day, technically, brings us one day closer to the grave. That obvious fact just never seemed particularly relevant when I was younger. Sure, every once in awhile I'd see an old person, squint my eyes and calculate that she used to be a young person. I'd mentally stretch her skin back and add some imaginary melanin, in order to try to concoct what she might have looked like and acted like at seven or eighteen or twenty-three. More often than not, though, I'd just go on with my business under the assumption that she'd simply been born old.

When I was eighteen, my mom lived adjacent to Los Angeles's famous Venice Beach. Most Americans have seen it in a lot of movies and television shows and music videos even if they don't realize they have. The boardwalk at Venice Beach was home to neighbors who were street artists, jugglers, dancers, palm readers, glass-shard walkers, fire eaters and hemp lobbyists. I'm still not entirely clear how the hemp lobbyists supported themselves.

One of the characters who rolled through Venice, Santa Monica and Malibu back in the day was Skating Grandma. Though we never met officially, I knew her name because she usually wore a sweatshirt that said "Skating Grandma." I'd guess she was around sixty-five years old. Skin weathered by the sun and gray hair sticking out from under a baseball cap, Skating Grandma seemed entirely comfortable wearing shiny, skin-tight, stretchy pants left over from the seventies. Some days she'd be on roller skates and other days she'd be skateboarding. If it was particularly windy, she'd be riding a long board with a sail, like a sailboat, through the parking lots. You can understand why this vibrant woman made such an impression on me.

At eighteen, strong and healthy, I actually *did* give that free-wheeling Grandma a good deal of consideration. Over the years I'd heard others make snide comments about older adults who "tried" to look or act young. I knew that many considered it a pretty grievous sin. I guess it did seem a little brazen, I reasoned, for someone *so old* to be wearing such shiny clothing. And skating around, so carefree. And unfettered. And alive. Didn't she realize how *old* she was? It seemed more than just a little offensive. It was as if Skating Grandma had, with her dress and lifestyle, single-handedly disrupted the natural order of things—which is saying a lot in Southern California.

I *wanted* to be offended by Grandma's blatant disregard for the proper ordering of society, but in my heart, I couldn't. This is because, at eighteen, I had already resigned myself to one given fact: there was no way on earth that I would stop roller skating or wearing gaudy clothes when I was sixty-five. Even at the time, I knew this would offend my eventual progeny. I knew that, whoever they'd be, they'd be a little embarrassed by me.

Today it's evident that I truly am on the precise trajectory to end up there, zooming along right beside Skating Grandma, by sixty-five. The horrified look on my daughter's face when I dressed up like an urban gangsta last year, to rap an announcement on her elementary school PA system, tells me it's already time to dial it back. When we're young, we want old people to do what they're supposed to do by getting old, failing to keep up with fashion, going gray, slowing down and eventually dying. Once we're old, we're completely opposed to the entire process.

What seems like a shame is that, in this battle between life and death, we're waging war with mascara wands, foil highlighting strips and tinfoil rapper bling. We're preserving the appearance of life, even as it slips away from us.

There has to be a better way.

A POSSIBILITY

Always one to make hair issues theological, I kept thinking about my friend's Facebook post about the difference between children's fabulous hair and the mousy stuff on adults who go natural. I hadn't ever realized that before—about kids having better hair than everyone else—but my friend Erica is a state-certified hairdressing professional, so I trusted her.

I couldn't help but muse that if this dulling-down phenomenon was the Creator's actual *design*, maybe there is a reason. Perhaps in some theologically orthodox aesthetic of beauty, there is some perfectly good reason for hair to lose its natural sheen over time.

Of course, it's not just the hair that goes. There are the wrinkles, the sagging skin, the loss of muscle tone, some extra bulges. I don't mean to be a bummer; it's just sort of the biological reality. So I can't help but wonder, about this predictable life-cycle pattern that most of us resent and resist, if there might not be some sort of divine rationale behind it.

For example, think about how completely yummy and attractive babies are. Babies attract the eye, the ear, the smell, the touch of their caregivers. Go ahead; take a moment to run through those. There are the beautifully proportioned features to delight the caregiver—big eyes, strangely large head-to-body ratio, and cute miniature fingers and toes. There are the cutie coos and endearing gurgling noises. There's the sweet way that babies smell—except when they really don't. And then there's the wonderfully satisfying comfort of holding a baby. From the soft little locks of their mostly bald heads, to their sweet squishy cheeks, to the smooth rolls of flesh on sometimes chunky little legs, it is almost impossible to *not* touch a baby. The same rolls we detest on forty-year-old thighs are absolutely scrumptious when glued to an infant. Seriously, if I'm around a sweet baby when I have a cold or some other contagious germ condition that prohibits me from reaching out and touching that kid, I just ask to be handcuffed. Otherwise, I just can't help myself. God did pretty well with that miniature package design, in terms of ability to attract attention, I think.

This is in the baby's best interest, of course, because the thing that a baby *most needs* is the attentive eye, ear, touch and care of the adults around her. Without that attention, she will not survive. Not only does she need the physical nurture of an adult caregiver; she also needs the adult's emotional presence. The wild attractiveness of infants, concocted by a pretty savvy Creator if you ask me, garners the attention of adults who can provide both sustenance and nurture.

The plan sort of begs the question: "Why do most of us start out our lives so irrefutably 'attractive' and then eventually sort of go downhill?" Especially when most of us still want all that same good stuff even as we get older?

THE TRAJECTORY

I'll tell you what I'm thinking. Children, by design, are egocentric. Developmentally, they're supposed to be. Not only do they naturally assume the world revolves around them, but they develop a sense of their identity in relationship to the trusted faces turned toward theirs. Ideally, these reflecting faces are healthy, nurturing adult ones.

As individuals mature, though, we expect them to become less egocentric. We expect the tantrums to stop. We expect that toys will be shared. We expect the individual who was once pretty absorbed with herself to begin to develop healthy relationships of mutuality and interdependence with others. That's what typical social development looks like.

Jesus, though, takes it a step further. Jesus expects his mature followers to do more than play well with others. Not only are we called to notice others and engage them; we're exhorted to be actively *for* them. Specifically, we're called to *lose* our own lives so that Jesus can live through us. Natural human development finds its ultimate end as individuals imitate Christ, who gave himself entirely *for* us.

Trust me when I promise I'm going to bring this back to the hair-coloring situation and the difficulties of aging in this youth- and beauty-obsessed culture.

Newborns, infants and children have an authentic developmental need to garner the attention of those around them. Their personal survival depends upon it. In addition, the survival of the race, which is no small thing, depends upon women and men of childbearing age attracting the attention of a mate.

As we age through and beyond those childbearing years, though, our bodies begin to suffer physical losses. Not only do we lose function, but we eventually lose the ability to turn heads with our youthful beauty. We lose the ability to attract attention with our physical appearance. Some of us who simply cannot bear this loss will manage our beauty situation so that we turn heads anyway: with our orange painted-on tans, our injected lips, and our surgically taut and frighteningly drawn faces.

So it's a little interesting that what's happening against our will—the dropping and sagging as we become gray, pale and frail—is what Jesus has essentially been inviting us to embrace all along, *with* our wills. If we really want to gain our lives, Jesus points out, we'll lose them. If we want to increase, we must decrease. If we want to be first, we must be last. If we want to live, we should die. If we want to attract God's good favor, we should give and pray and fast in ways that don't attract the good favor of others here and now. According to Jesus' kingdom logic, then, it only makes sense that if we want to be seen, we should see. If we want to be heard, we should listen. If we want to be loved, we should love.

Although I realize that this still probably sounds less than inspiring, I see real promise for those of us who want to age with grace.

THE MOVEMENT INTO MATURITY

While we begin our visit to this planet entirely self-referenced, Jesus invites his followers into a kingdom way of life where we become other-referenced, turning our gaze from our own navels and tipping it toward God and others. The overarching spiritual movement into which we're continually called by Jesus, both in our youth and in advanced age, is one in which we take our eyes off of ourselves and turn them upon God and others. For useful prooftexts, please refer to the entire New Testament.

Christians are called to give our lives *for* others. Perhaps losing the ability to garner lots and lots of attention for ourselves, with our captivating youthful appearances, will help form us toward that end. That said, I'm more than willing to entertain the possibility that this logic might be trying too hard to look on the bright side.

The prophet Isaiah describes God's suffering servant: "He had no beauty or majesty to attract us to him, / nothing in his appearance that we should desire him" (Isaiah 53:2). I'm not sure it's very useful to dwell too much on the physical attractiveness of God's chosen one, but it's interesting to note that dashing-politician-good-looks weren't requisite.

I don't think it's *entirely* irrelevant that the one we were created to desire, the one most worthy of human love and attention, displayed nothing in his own appearance that would attract us to him. Although our culture esteems the kind of appearances that turn heads, Jesus actually exhorts his followers to practice piety in ways that are decidedly unnoticeable! So though I'm sure the bland, pictureless, academic theological journals of the day would have featured Jesus, we never would have seen him on the cover of *People* or *Us* or *Rolling Stone*.

Instead of attracting us with the good looks, there was something else about this guy that drew people to himself. There was something about the way he moved through the world. This is certainly true in my own encounter with Christ. His gaze and his ear were already tilted in my direction. I didn't have to tap him on the shoulder to get his attention, or get all dolled up, or make any embarrassing phone call I'd later regret. What attracted me to Jesus was finding out that, in his sacrificial love, he was already *for* me. He had already demonstrated bodily, in his living and in his dying, that he was altogether *for* me. That's the thing for which we were made as well—giving our attention, giving our selves, *for* others.

Though we crave the admiring glances of others, though we long to attract attention, though we long to be found attractive, we were made to notice others.

I'm not saying that those of us who might be declining in our ability to attract attention, if we ever had much of that going on anyway, don't have the regular, everyday human needs for relationship. I wouldn't dare. I'm just saying that those needs won't necessarily be met by naturally, or desperately, attracting lots of attention to ourselves. These needs may be met, however, as we do the thing we were made to do in the first place: love God and love others. As we're released from our clawing need to garner attention for ourselves, purposing to offer loving attention to others—regardless of age, race, class and ability—we find that our own need for love is met.

The life of Jesus, in us, reorients our identity and purpose so that we need not find our lives in the admiring glances of others. Instead, we lose our lives—the way we were made to—as our eyes look in love upon others, reflecting *their* worth.

It's really an interesting situation, that.

23

JUSTICE

From Doritos to Discipleship

Every so often, while waiting in the school carpool line and mentally planning my grocery list, I remember to be dismayed that I live on a small planet where millions of us struggle to manage our obesity and many millions more go hungry every night.

I never cease to find this absurd.

Or I'll be throwing my entire body weight against my overstuffed shirt drawer to squeeze it shut, stumbling a little over extraneous shoes I've left lying around, and I'll remember that children around the globe are living entirely shoeless, shirtless.

There has simply got to be a way to do some better sharing.

And though I understand that sharing resources isn't quite as simple as wrapping my Ben & Jerry's Half-Baked pint in brown paper and shipping it to central Africa, or dropping a few shirts off at Goodwill, I do think that a Christian worldview informs the choices Americans make about bodies and food and clothes.

Or, rather, it was *meant* to.

The ways we spend our money and the ways we spend our time, caring for our bodies, matters.

Believe me, I say that with more than a little fear and trembling. If you're addicted to chocolate or shopping or Diet Coke or shoes, I'm going to recommend that you tremble a little bit with me too.

RELUCTANT DISCIPLE

I don't want the way I care for my body—what my body uses and consumes—to matter. I want it to be one of those issues that the New Testament calls *adiaphora*, or "indifferent." I want it to be stuff that doesn't really matter, like choosing between a Sponge-Bob Band-Aid or a Scooby-Doo one at the doctor's office. I don't want bodily consumption—of food, drink, clothes, shampoo, jewelry, cigarettes, alcohol, drugs, makeup—to matter.

The reason I don't want it to matter is because I don't exactly have my act together.

Unfortunately, I know what it is to void a vending machine of all its Reese's Peanut Butter Cups and to quickly scarf down those anxiety-reducing happy-disks in secret. I know what it is to slide a fizzy carbonated sugar beverage into my shopping cart, even though I know good and well that I'm throwing my money down the drain on those useless, non-nutritive things. I know what it is to make an unnecessary purchase at Marshalls, for 40 percent less than I would have at another major retailer, and then feel a little sickish when that fantastic thing ends up sitting in my closet, unworn, because it just hasn't changed my life the way I thought it might. Trust me, I get it. I understand how much effort it takes for people of privilege to not use our resources for our own comforts. I get that.

So when I say that the way we care for our bodies matters, I'm not trying to pass judgment about having too many shoes or being pleasantly plump or having overflowing drawers. I've found myself—and continue to find myself—in all of these embarrassing situations. Rather, I want to elevate the whole discussion about our bodies and the care of them from denim and Doritos to discipleship. I want us to think about how being followers of Jesus affects the ways we utilize the resources with which we've been entrusted.

Really, if you think about it, it's not a very big stretch. It's not so very unreasonable to believe that our lives have an impact on others—those inextricably bound to us by virtue of their belovedness to the Father we share—who are naked, hungry and poor. I'm pretty sure Jesus mentioned this very thing once or twice.

Too often, though, I can go about my day pretty mindless of these ones whom God loves.

EATING FOR JESUS

One way our family purposes to meet our needs while also holding the needs of the poor in our hearts is by eating a simple meal of rice and beans each week. For many parents around the world, having rice and beans to put on the family table is cause for thanksgiving. When I do it, I fear mutiny.

The scene rarely varies. At the end of a hard day's work, my husband strides through the front door and naively queries, "What's for dinner?"

Quietly, as if to soften the blow, I choke out, "Rice and beans."

He keeps a stiff upper lip, but I know he's disappointed.

Overhearing this, my eldest demands, "Is that *it?*" as if she's expecting a side of caviar.

Bravely, I confirm, "Yup, that's it."

My middle son reacts as if I've just announced that I'll be frying up a vat of cockroach larvae.

Disgusted, he moans in agony, "Awww! I *hate* rice and beans!"

"Yeah," I say wryly. "I remember from last week."

Finally, there is the award-winning performance by my youngest, "Hooray! Rice and beans! It's my *favorite!*" I can't even *enjoy* the NFL celebration dance because the prancing and shouting is meant only to get a rise out of his frustrated siblings.

Without fail, it does.

When I first suggested the modest meal a few years ago, I was surprised when my husband readily agreed. I would later realize we were imagining two different things.

In my mind, the idea was to limit our freedom of choice as the world's poor are daily forced to do. For just one meal we would get by on rice, beans and water. The less flavor, the better—that's what I always say.

My groom saw it all differently. He felt certain that even impoverished providers would find a way to salvage a little oil, an onion and perhaps some curry to make the best possible showing with their limited resources.

That is one slippery slope.

One week it's a dash of cumin, and the next thing you know we're serving sides of cheese and tortillas. I put my foot down at margaritas. Somewhere along the way we had confused the simple solidarity meal with the menu at our favorite Mexican restaurant. Thankfully, we came to our senses. I could take or leave the spices, but it was tough saying *adiós* to the cheese.

When I failed to clean my plate as a child, I heard: "Think of the starving children in _____" (fill in the blank: India, China, Africa). In my home today, the age-old threat takes on a whole new twist. My youngest son, adopted, was *born* in India. Though he's clearly happy enough to eat his rice and beans, I'm certain he would jump at the opportunity to box up some asparagus and ship it off to his buddies in Southeast Asia.

What my family fails to grasp is that I don't *want* to tell them that it's rice and beans night. Do they imagine that *I* relish the bland staples? Do they think I *enjoy* torturing them?

On most days, I don't.

In fact, recent polls show hot dogs or macaroni could garner me a 50 percent approval rating. Better yet, I could bellow, "Candy bars! Cola! Banana splits! Don't bother washing your hands; just come to the table!"

I fancy the thought that I would be the most popular mom on the block.

Now, once a week I am reminded of Jesus' words: "Blessed are those who are persecuted because of righteousness, / for theirs is the kingdom of heaven" (Matthew 5:10).

The righteous are *never* the most popular moms on the block.

Ten Ideas for Food Discipleship

1. *If you're not hungry, don't eat.*

2. *Once you've started eating, stop when you're no longer hungry.*

3. *Eat slowly. It takes about twenty minutes for the brain to receive signals that the stomach is full. The real beauty there is that God's good gift of sharing fellowship around a table with others seems to have been sort of built into the original product design.*

4. *Reconsider the beverages you drink. Consider replacing costly, sugary juice drinks with water and actual fruits and veggies.*

5. *When you're grocery shopping, eliminate some of the unnecessary items that mysteriously jump into your shopping cart: gum, soda pop, Oreos, malted milk balls, etc. (All the fun stuff, I know.)*

6. *While shopping, just say no to products with lots of excess packaging and ones that offer free toys inside each box. I promise you: they're not free.*

7. *Fast, on behalf of others, for a meal or a day.*

8. *Avoid red meat for a month in favor of grains, which use fewer resources to nourish our bodies. Maybe try eating rice and beans one night each week. If you have friends who'd be up for that—and I really hope you do—invite them over to share it. Check out Willow Creek's Celebration of Hope challenge at <www.willowcreek.org/coh> for other ideas of what the world's poor are eating.*

9. *Grow something edible in your backyard: tomatoes, lettuce, chicken eggs. (Be warned: eating the chickens is really going to make a dent in egg production.)*

10. *Eat gratefully. When you eat, give thanks for what you have and pray for those in need.*

EATING LEFTOVERS

The disappointment in my performance doesn't end there. I wish it did, but there's always the leftovers situation. I'm not even talking about the slim rice and bean leftovers; even the leftovers from a prior carnivorous evening can elicit fuming and fussing.

Whenever we don't have a fresh, new, surprising meal in the fridge, Peter or I will quickly get a hankering to go out to a restaurant. The bill for our family of five can tally anywhere from twelve dollars at Taco Bell to almost forty bucks at the all-you-can-eat buffet. The gluttonous buffet, of course, is too morally dicey to be given proper treatment here in these pages. It really needs its own volume.

The leftovers in our fridge, of course, are free. Free food. We paid for it originally, but next to the buffet, it *feels* free. Though this logic holds absolutely no sway with my children, either Peter or I, in our best moments, will gently remind the other: *free food.*

That said, I'm not at all convinced there's any particular moral good in scoring a financial bargain from the fridge, or Walmart, or the J.Crew catalog. Though thrift is fine, this is one of those places where I think that it's what's in the heart, not what's in the bank, that matters. (Really, is it ever?) I don't think that God is particularly impressed that I can come home from the store with three pairs of name-brand pants for under twelve dollars. And yes, I've done it. If that just means I've got more money in the bank or more money to invest or more money to spend on an insane impulsive irresponsible whim, it's hardly impressive. Don't even get me started on "saving" money by shopping at stores that don't treat their workers fairly. Believe me, *someone* has paid the price, and it's usually them.

A few years ago a friend gave me *The Better World Shopping Guide* as a Christmas gift. I think it goes without saying that she's one of those friends on the journey for whom I'm pretty grateful. The handy pocket reference is a convenient way to identify grocery stores, gas stations, clothing manufacturers and other providers with a commitment to human rights, the environment, animal protection, community involvement and social justice. It also notes the ones who are committed to turning a big greedy profit at the express expense of all these. It's what finally helped me understand the value of paying a little more for something in pursuit of the greater good of others. It opened my eyes to see that, more often than not, insanely ridiculous bargains are, as a rule, pretty much for my own personal benefit. And while, in recent years, I've been a little politically dubious about Americans spending lots of money on ourselves to stimulate the economy, I really can get behind the idea of spending a little extra for things we actually need that have been made by folks treated justly for their labor. As Christians, our choices have simply *got* to be bigger than ourselves.

For instance, if Peter talks reluctant me into eating last night's dry chicken because he wants us to be responsible stewards of the kingdom resources that have been entrusted to us, I am entirely obligated to consider that unsavory situation. That sort of reasoning is bigger than choosing not to eat a meal out at a restaurant in order to greedily make more of our financial resources available to us to buy more junk. I have to think God smiles on a kind of diet that purposes to love others, both those in my kitchen I'm trying to nourish and those far away who desperately need nourishment. I know it sounds totally dull and uninspired from a culinary point of view, but from the discipleship angle, I think disappointing leftovers are one of the most exciting things going.

Though there doesn't seem to be a single English word for this kind of acknowledgment of others that drives behavior, Bishop Desmond Tutu has articulated for the world an African cultural value called *ubuntu*. What *ubuntu* articulates is that human beings do not exist in isolation. One English translation is, "I am because we are and because we are, I am." Tutu explains, "A person with *ubuntu* is welcoming, hospitable, warm and generous, willing to share." Specifically, the person with *ubuntu* understands that she is inextricably bound to others. Tutu continues, "They know that they are diminished when others are humiliated, diminished when others are oppressed, diminished when others are treated as if they were less than who they are."[1]

The more I chew on that good stuff, the more convinced I am that there's a lot to be said for an *ubuntu*-like interdependence. Followers of Jesus simply can*not* live only unto ourselves.

ONE HUNDRED YARDS
Recently I stumbled upon an eating adventure even more titillating than the leftovers.

One of my regular writing gigs is being the confessions editor for *Geez* magazine's "Sinner's Corner." And how fun is that? Readers write in to share those temptations that threaten to woo them from living a life of love and justice. For example, the first time I rode a four-wheeler, on a weekend trip to a friend's mountain home, I suddenly found myself wanting to own a four-wheeler. And a mountain. In my mind, those who live lives of simplicity and sacrifice would come to the mountain to be refreshed, enjoy the four-wheeler and then return back to the trenches to live an austere life of love. My mind is such a funny place to be sometimes.

So, the fun of being the confessions editor, of course, is that I get to hear people's various temptations. Some of these involve

---

[1]Desmond Tutu, *God Has a Dream: A Vision of Hope for Our Time* (New York: Doubleday, 2005), p. 26.

Walmart, whiskey flasks, curse words and cruise liners.

One recent confession really blew my socks off. I believe I can honor my confessional obligation to anonymity—among those of you who aren't subscribers—by hiding the confessor's identity. The woman writing explained that she and her family lived on what she called a one-hundred-yard diet. I was familiar with the one-hundred-mile diet: eating only food that has been grown, raised and produced within one hundred miles of one's home. The jacked-up version of one hundred miles, of course, for eco-superheroes, is the one-hundred-yard diet. Amazing, huh?

Now, here comes her confession. You may want to brace yourself. A local grocer had given her leftover produce scraps to feed her chickens. These weren't one-hundred-yard scraps; they were just the usual kind flown in from Argentina and Bolivia. If they hadn't become chicken feed, they'd have ended up at the dump. The confessor, though, had picked through these produce scraps, pulling out plump juicy grapes and strawberries and greens, to feed her family. And therein lies the ethical dilemma. Should she and her family have eaten food that they wouldn't otherwise purchase in a gazillion years? The burden with which she'd been living was the morality of eating trash.

Isn't that the most awesome ethical dilemma you've ever heard of? Her sin puts my very best not-sinning days to shame. For the record, that wasn't meant to shame anyone who wouldn't be caught dead eating trash. It was simply an inspirational tidbit.

I'm real clear that everybody's journey with Jesus looks different. In fact, most of us reading this book will complete our earthly journey with Jesus and will still have eaten no trash. I simply suspect that he is inviting each of us, increasingly, to dress, groom, eat and drink with justice in mind.

24

MINDFULNESS

Why I'm *Most* Jazzed
About My Fabulous Couch Pants

A few years back, my friend Lola was all excited about a brand-new television show she thought I'd be *great* on. Sure I'd be a hit, she encouraged me to apply. Flattered, I secretly hoped it was something fabulous like *Ellen*. Or *Soul Train*. I asked her what the show was. In the same happy breath in which she told me it was called *What Not to Wear*, she generously offered to help me through the application process.

She did not even flinch when she said that mean thing.

Though I'd not yet seen the show, I could put the pieces together to realize it probably wasn't a compliment. Anyone with cable television today will note that my keen instincts were right on the mark. Don't worry; there were no hard feelings involved. I did not apply for the show, and we have continued to be friends.

FUNCTION OVER FASHION
No one has ever accused me of being too fashion-conscious. I

am much more concerned with function.

For as long as I can remember, I've thought to myself things such as the following:

What if I suddenly had to parachute out of an airplane into a remote jungle wilderness terrain? If I happened to be wearing spike heels and contact lenses that day, there's no question that before long I'd end up unable to see and I'd have a broken ankle. All the jungle natives would take one look at me and exchange knowing glances among themselves that I was obviously about to become lion bait.

If I were wearing unstylish sneakers and thick glasses, however, I wouldn't look great, but I'm certain I'd survive longer than I would in the stilettos and contacts. I'd live way longer in a jungle or the desert or an unplanned trip to Mars. Should any of those situations occur today.

This is how it's always gone in my mind.

Although I probably do deserve my own entire spin-off of *What Not to Wear*, I find it a little disturbing that most of us aren't making *more* clothing choices based on function. Whether we're wide-hipped or thick-waisted or slender-butted, too many of us are choosing clothes simply on the basis of whether or not they make our bodies *look* good. Think about that. We hobble around in painful high-heeled shoes or wear tight skirts we can't actually run in or don tailored jackets that don't allow us to throw a football. It seems like the *shoes* women wear are some of the worst offenders. We squeeze our feet into footwear that looks fantastic and then live with corns, bunions and pain throughout all our unsupported tendons and ligaments.

I'm not advocating that women wear sweats and sneakers every day to work and school and church and weddings, but I would like us to ask a few more questions about this fashion situation than we've asked up to this point. Our big rationale for the painful footwear has been our insistence that we dress up so that we'll *feel* good. I just want women to own the fact we'd all actually feel *better* in sensible shoes.

MODESTY

There's really no clear rule of thumb today about how a "Christian woman" might dress. The term no longer carries any shared assumption about fashion or propriety or modesty. In fact, many of us have discarded, as somewhat antiquated, responsibility for the ways in which our exposed breasts, abs and thighs arouse the random man toward lustfulness. As is our way, we find clever justification to rationalize our plunging necklines, tight knits and high hems. Really, we're geniuses with this stuff.

Although we may be able to justify it up and down, the fact is that we choose to do it because it does something for us. Like my three-year-old daughter had discovered before strangely exposing her sweet round belly, we *do* gain something when we use our bodies to attract a particular kind of attention. Esteem? Power? Perceived value? It might be easier for us to really get at what we gain with our sexy duds if we turn it around. What would we *lose* should we, perchance, decide to suddenly start dressing like our grandmothers? Esteem? Power? Perceived value? Nothing keeps it real like dressing like one's own grandmother.

I'm not saying we have to go there. For some of us, that would be a very scary, polyester, mothball-smelling place to be. We do need to fess up, though, about whether our could-be-on-MTV outfits facilitate our bodies being *for* ourselves or *for* others.

Top Ten Reasons to Smirk at Antiquated Suggestions of Modesty

1. *It's the style.*
   This is how the clothes are made. It's not like I whipped out my Singer sewing machine, cut a pattern and stitched these up myself. They came this way.

2. It's not that bad.
It's not like anything is going to fall out. If there's no bending, walking or sitting involved, it's all mostly covered.

3. There's a lot worse out there.
Have you seen what the pastor's daughter wears?!?!

4. I'm a mother.
For heaven's sake, I'm not some young coed. Who's going to be attracted to sweet innocent li'l ole me?

5. It makes me feel good.
I wear this because when I do, I feel feminine.

6. It's not hurting anyone.
No one's ever mentioned to me that they are challenged by lusting after my body, so it's probably not even an issue.

7. It's the same thing everyone else is wearing.
Even if I wasn't wearing this, someone else would be.

8. It's what's on the inside that counts, not what's on the outside.
I think that possibly you are the superficial one for even noticing my plunging neckline. Cuz it's what's on the inside that really counts.

9. It's the twenty-first century.
I'm pretty sure that high collars and low hemlines went out of style a few centuries ago.

10. God made it, so I'll flaunt it.
Can I even help it if I look this great?

Being *for* others was exactly what New Testament Paul was about when he made the distinction between personal preferences that really were indifferent and the ones that would cause others to sin. Private choices that invite others into sin are *precisely* the points at which we must set aside our own preferences in order to be *for* others. Believe me, even as I hear myself exhorting women toward something that could be perceived as buttoning up and lengthening down, I can *hear* how corny and outdated it sounds. After all, we're modern women.

Guys, though? They've still got the same old brains.

Unfortunately, I don't hear Christian women having a lot of conversations about how we are to dress. Sure, we'll rave if a friend has cute shoes or we'll fawn over her new jewelry, but we don't often dig in to harder conversations about how disciples of Jesus think about the necessary act of clothing ourselves. We know all about the helmet of salvation, the breastplate of righteousness and the peace sandals. We might even look in the mirror and prayerfully don that armor every single morning. Or, if we're feeling particularly self-righteous, we might choose to cast a judging eye on teens at church who wear frighteningly tight-fitting clothes. If we do decide to do that, let's go ahead and start with the tight tees decorated with pink rhinestone crucifixes glued on by underpaid Third World laborers. (Whoops! See how quickly I got off of style and onto other disturbing matters?)

I'm convinced, though, that God invites us to meet this most basic human need in a way that honors him.

This is big.

I'm willing to admit that we probably even need to dig deeper than whether or not we're able to shimmy up a tall thin tree while being chased by a ravenous jungle beast. Specifically, let's talk about where we shop, how often we shop, what we buy and how much we spend.

Oh yeah, I went there.

SPENDING

As a child, I hated shopping for clothes. I despised riding in the cart or standing behind my mother as she pawed through endless racks at the Marshalls on Roosevelt Road. Given my druthers, I would have been climbing a domestic tree in my backyard, get-

ting sap on my shirt and ripping my pants on a branch. Adults
just don't know how to wear out clothes like children do. I've tried
to wear out my clothes, as an adult, and the closest I've gotten is
some dangerously stained armpits.

When I was a child, my mom and grandmother would sneak
new clothing into my wardrobe under the guise of *Christmas gift*
or *birthday gift*—an absolutely outrageous violation of the terms,
in my opinion. But there was one annual shopping trip that I
knew could not be avoided: the trip for back-to-school clothes.
Whatever marketer came up with those three magic words was
an absolute genius.

I can almost see the advertising execs sitting around the board-
room, musing, "If we can just brainwash these people to believe
that there's no possible way that what they wore on August 29 or
August 31 can actually be worn again to school during the first
three weeks of September, we'll be golden." That devilish scheme
turned out to be such a big success, of course, that today retailers
selling everything from Elmer's Glue to leather couches have gotten on board with it. Now, once a year, they've got the American
public marveling, "Hmmm, I probably *do* need to buy some back-
to-school dental floss . . ."

When the back-to-school schtick proved so effective, retailers
started drumming up an entirely new line of clothes *every* fall,
every winter, *every* spring and *every* summer. Heck, the marketing
strategy worked so well that eventually Old Navy started carrying seasonal holiday tees to be worn *one* day of the year. *One day*,
people. Now other retailers have caught on, and selling clothing
for the minor holidays that feature hearts, clovers and flags is all
the rage.

I think it goes without saying that, with a few exceptions, the
clothes being hocked today are of pretty poor quality. Though
this stinks for consumers, it's a win-win-win situation for retailers. Laborers who *create* the clothes are paid horribly low wages,
the people who *sell* them get no health benefits, and the people

who *buy* them—that's us—will be back in a few months to buy more because the first ones have fallen apart. I welcome you to find this whole situation entirely infuriating with me.[1]

I have dared to fantasize that it might be different.

Though I don't usually shop at malls, on occasion I'll be cutting through Sears or JCPenney or Macy's or Belk to get somewhere really important, like a restaurant that serves mini-cheeseburgers. On my way I typically marvel at the sheer volume of merchandise that I know will soon be replaced by new merchandise. In a lot of malls, it will be sold. In the mall by my home, which is usually pretty vacant, I'm just not sure where the clothes go.

During these moments I have a fantasy that's a little odd for someone who loves stripes and polka dots and colors so much. In this fantasy, I wonder: *What if this store did not generate new styles each season, with sort-of-new patterns in ever-so-slightly new colors and, instead, stocked some sensible, sturdy clothing that would last for a while?*

I know the answer. We all do. That store would go down the tubes in a heartbeat. For a while it seemed like that might actually have been the marketing strategy of Sears and JCPenney—until they came to their profit-driven senses, that is, and started running ads like Target and Walmart that promised something new and wonderful and happy-making and different every time you went to the store.

Can't you see I've got their number, though? I am *on* to them. These guys don't even fool me for a second.

RESISTANCE

Though advertisers insist on barraging us with terribly happy models wearing these stylish clothes on carnival rides and playgrounds, and while river-rafting and sharing secrets with their close friends over a cup of coffee, we simply have to resist the

---

[1]Check out <www.StoryofStuff.com> for actual facts about this whole deal.

manipulative lie that satisfaction can be bought for $14.88 at Walmart.

Sorry if that sounded a little strident. I just think this is pretty important. Women buy into this lie, quite literally, when we attempt to keep up with every changing fashion. When we buy new clothes every few months, telling ourselves that *these* are the ones we'll really wear for years and years because they're so perfect, when our closets are already stuffed, we perpetuate a lie. Believe me, I know of what I speak.

One of the styles I mistakenly tried to keep in step with for a few years was capri pants. One year they were hot, and the next year, not. Then the third year they were hot again. This absolutely infuriated me. *I'll show them,* I vowed. On one of the off years, I bought some capris at a crazy end-of-summer bargain sale. Then I cut off the legs at the knee, sewed in an extra ten-inch swatch of flowery fabric and *voilà!* They were pants again. Pants that could be worn for years. I really showed them.

For the record, making additional purchases to really teach those retailers a lesson is not a strategy I want to endorse. It was an emergency.

Another act of radical consumer defiance is one for which I can't really take credit. I have a few cozy fleece sweatshirts that I wear every day between October and March. I wear the pink one when I'm clean, and I wear the unfortunate-hue-of-green one when I plan to sweat. (It was a bad year for green at Lands' End.) I wear them every day because they're cozy and they keep me warm and I love them. So it's hard to really take credit for something so smart that is also so satisfying. Still, the fact that they've each had over a thousand wears is something I'm a little pleased with. No young girl has ever looked at happy me, by golly, and deduced that she needs to buy the most recent fashions to keep up. I try to inspire.

Consider buying secondhand clothes. I know this can seem a little off-putting to some, but just think about trying it. Some of my most fabulous pants are brown corduroy pants from Goodwill with a panel of just-the-right-color green and brown decorator couch fabric I stitched on at the bottom. I get more compliments on those three-dollar pants than on anything else I own. And although the garnering of compliments isn't what I want to promote here, I do want to emphasize that the thoughtful use of resources can be more fun—and *stylish*—than most people would think it might be.

I'm aware that many will find the picture I've painted here of capri extensions, elbow-worn fleeces and couch pants pretty unsavory. Every woman must find her own way. There's an opportunity here, though, for *each* of us to practice bold, frugal following after Jesus.

25

AUTHENTICITY

B Who U R

The other evening I was walking through my neighborhood when a friend, who teaches ethics at Duke Divinity School, spotted me just as she was opening the door to welcome a dinner guest.

"Margot!" she shouted. "I was just *thinking* about you!"

Well, that always makes a person feel good.

Hollering across the street, she continued on to describe how she had been scurrying around the house, scrambling to clean it up for weekend guests. Finally, she explained, she had stopped in the middle of all the frantic cleaning and said to herself, *What would Margot do?*

You read that correctly. The Duke University ethics professor asked herself, *What would* Margot *do?* I can almost see it now, imprinted on a neon rubber bracelet. For a nanosecond, I felt special and fantastic. Possibly a little holy.

As soon as my brain was able to process what she was saying, though, I felt less fantastic. What she was actually saying was, *If*

Margot had company coming over to her messy house, would she clean it up? No! She wouldn't bother! That lazy gal would just let them walk in on the usual visual chaos in which her family lives every single day. I deduced, from my friend's happy smile, that I had just inspired her to mediocrity as well.

I do what I can. Though the neat freaks are probably horrified, I suspect the slobs secretly relish coming to my house.

It's the same with bodies. We blather on, "Sorry you have to look at this head; I'm having a bad hair day. A bad hair month. When I'm having my period, I get all these zits. Do you like my muffin top? I've *got* to start working out. Does my butt look big in these jeans? Ugh, I hate these thigh dimples. I didn't used to have these . . ."

Isn't it just exhausting?

We leave no room to notice and welcome others when we ramble on and on about our particular disappointments with our appearances. Not only that, but as we do, we reveal to other women what it is we value. We may not mean to, but we do. When we bring it up, we confirm that we agree with the world's valuing of us and, ultimately, we agree with the world's valuing of them.

COMFORTABLE

In case it wasn't obvious, I suspect the converse is also true. When we don't highlight our imperfections, we subvert the world's twisty values. I'm not saying this simply because my grandmother instructed me, as a girl, to never draw attention to features I don't like about myself. My theory is based on actual research.

I've conducted a few informal studies to learn more about the kind of women about whom people say, "She's comfortable in her own skin." You know the ones. I suspect you like to be around them very much. What I've found is that this isn't said about a lot of supermodels or Hollywood divas or famous female rock stars. More often, I hear it spoken about women who *aren't* glamorously beautiful. For instance, I've heard it said about a very elderly woman who's full of life and zest. I've heard it said about a woman who is actively involved in community service and is overweight. I've heard it said about someone who takes a keen interest in others and just doesn't happen to fit the world's mold of beauty.

Specifically, it's said about women who don't do this tiring thing with going on and on about their imperfections. They don't *deny* their imperfections; they just don't expend a whole lot of energy drawing attention to them. Like my grandmother suggested.

That's it. That's the whole strategy. By not wasting any energy on noticing their less-than-perfectness, these women confirm that they are good enough.

I pray that *good enough* is just as contagious as *not good enough*.

DESPERATE

Though I'm not one bit proud to admit it, on Sunday night I watched *Desperate Housewives*. *Shame, shame*, I know. If any woman in her thirties or forties who is an actual housewife—or career professional, for that matter—is in the mood to feel really bad after comparing her body to others, her TiVoed episode of *Desperate Housewives* should be the first stop. Visually, those women have got it going on. The rest of their lives is a twisted web of mayhem, pain and deception, but they really do look good.

Hear me out. In a completely unexpected turn of events, the writers of *Desperate Housewives* actually told the truth about bodies and beauty. Tom Scavo, Lynette's husband, is interviewing for a job. He's discouraged because he's been losing jobs to younger men. Impressed by a more youthful-looking peer who'd had plastic surgery, Tom decides to have his face "done."

It was Lynette's logic that really grabbed me. She'd tried the old "You'll look ridiculous," and it hadn't swayed her husband at all. Then she said that, as the two of them aged together, she wanted them to *match*. That one was not bad. When she finally got honest about it, though, she said, in essence, "If you think that *you* need it, then one day you'll look at me and think that *I* need it." If you're dissatisfied with you, then you'll be dissatisfied with me. If you're dissatisfied with your humanness, you'll be dissatisfied with mine.

Lynette Scavo had hit the nail right on the head. I suspect that Tom could have, and would have, told her that her aging body was beautiful until the cows came home, but that sort of pep talk is sort of hard to believe coming from someone with artificially tight facial skin who—clearly—doesn't believe it.

CLEAR

Whether or not we've had "work" done, we do send pretty clear signals to others about whether or not we really believe that our bodies are acceptable just as they are. Those around us are naturally clever enough to do the math to deduce whether or not we find them acceptable.

A friend of mine teaches at a local university. Having decided that the way God had made her was *good*, this vibrant black woman wears her kinky black hair "natural," choosing not to straighten it or wear hair extensions. She confides that a number of her students have approached her privately to learn more about her decision. Though also inclined to go "natural," these young women, who are entering the ranks of professionals in the academy and the business world and the church, fear that such a decision will negatively affect their career options.

The message that my professor friend sends, with her quiet choices, is that what God has made is good. Really, you don't need a Ph.D. to model this stuff. Each one of us has the power to influence other women and girls. As we reject the world's hiss that we're not good enough, we proclaim a message of freedom for others caught in the world's sticky Cover Girl web. As you decide to accept your body as *good*, you authorize other women to do the same. I don't mean that in some idealized dimension other women might possibly notice and then *maybe* try being okay with their bodies. I mean that this is precisely where the rubber hits the road today. This is exactly the point at which a gospel of unconditional acceptance is being realized on campuses, in boardrooms and in the marketplace.

GOOD LEADERS

All of us who have the opportunity to be leaders of women, role models for girls and friends to our friends owe them this much. (If you don't find yourself in that list, you're just not paying attention.) This morning I was absolutely delighted when I found an online photo of a woman who happens to be a popular Christian speaker. In the picture she was looking particularly . . . real.

"Hooray!" I hollered, to no one other than myself. I felt so happy that she looked like people really look, with the hair and the face and the outfit and the body. The fact that I know other women are already looking toward her, because of her professional role, made me imagine her as sort of a superhero woman who liberates those enslaved to hair dyes and diet pills and overly pricey shampoos.

If I ever see her in person, I sort of want to go up and hug her and tell her how thrilled I am that she looks so normal and not particularly fantastic. In fact, what I really want to do is give her a trophy. And others like her. I'd like to establish the annual "Keeping It Real" awards for daring women who bravely break out of the world's mold. It would be sort of like being crowned Miss America, only more like Miss *Not*-America. Maybe instead of a crown I could just give out a sparkly baseball cap to hide the bad hair.

The first year, I imagine, these awards might not carry a lot of prestige. But what if it caught on? What if high-profile women, and low-profile ones, even started competing for it?! One day they'd skip the lipstick, the next month they might miss an appointment to touch up their roots. Before you know it, they might even switch to wearing sensible shoes. Can you imagine *People* magazine featuring a pair of women, dressed in the same comfortable outfit, and instead of a caption demanding "Who wore it better?" it would read, "Who kept it real?" Before you knew it, we might have an army of women walking around looking like we really look.

The first person I'd nominate would be my friend Constance. As part of the True Campaign, she went a month without makeup, posting a new plain beautiful photo every day on Facebook. I have to believe that that radical little experiment did more to help women than all the unbelievable reassurances in the world that God doesn't care how you look.

I'm of the mind that this sort of thing needs to happen more often than it does. Girls and women need role models who walk the talk. I don't just mean women who speak in front of thousands at Women of Faith conferences or ones who strut down a Parisian catwalk. We need to lay eyes on teachers, bus drivers, doctors, accountants, pastors, mothers, custodians and clerks who set us free by keeping it real.

MAE

A number of years ago, one of my walking friends was Mae. When Mae and I walked together, I was always aware that I sort of faded into a dark mass beside the radiant aura of Mae's wild beauty. I'm not exaggerating. When guys passed us and I looked into their mirrored sunglasses tilted toward Mae, I could see that she basked in a radiant halo of light. I could also see a shadowy blob next to her. That was me.

What's weird was that I was completely fine with this phenomenon. I truly was. I knew that if I were walking by myself, I would have had my own glowing aura. I'm not saying it would have been an Academy Awards red-carpet aura, but it was pretty joyful. My aura says, "I'm pretty happy to be me." It gets even a little bigger if I have earplugs stuck in my head playing Earth, Wind & Fire. Put me on roller skates and that thing becomes totally unwieldy. I'm not trying to be braggy about it; I'm just explaining

why I'm so entirely fine being a shadowy blob of a specimen next
to my gorgeous friend.

I'm good enough the way I am.

STOP THE MADNESS

We can also chip away at some of the culture's craziness about
women and beauty when we make the effort to know, *really* know,
the stories of other women. There is real power when we tell one
another the truth about our experiences.

I confess that as I was drawn into thinking and praying and
speaking and writing about beauty, I felt pretty uncomfortable
presuming to say anything meaningful about the bodily experience of the many women whose experiences are different than
my own. I couldn't. So I didn't.

That's the sinister hiss that kept me silent for too long. If I
couldn't speak meaningfully about the experience of *all* women,
including those from cultures different than mine, who move
through the world in differently abled bodies and differently colored skins, I didn't really have much to say about women's bodies. How could I? So I kept my narrow pink lips shut.

As I listened to a diverse group of friends, though, the wily
double bind became apparent. *None* of us have experienced the
world in any way *other* than the skin we are in. Duh. So to allow
single-toned-ness or any other determining factor to be a disqual-
ifier for naming what's wrong with our culture's insistence on a
particular brand of physical attractiveness is sort of crazy logic.

On the other hand, if we conspire together, we begin to chip
away at the world's lies about women and beauty. Together, in
conversation with one another, we get at what's really happening in our culture and in our heads. As we listen to one another,
we start to recognize familiar patterns of thinking that insist
that the way we've been made isn't quite right. We find we're
hearing very *similar* messages hissing that we'd be more attractive if we looked like someone other than who we are.

There is power in crossing these boundaries. Although I didn't have these kinds of conversations with friends when I was in high school, I wish I had. I learned that one Korean friend, who I reconnected with as an adult, and who was raised by parents and grandparents who'd endured the poverty of war, was actually encouraged to become chubbier! This dreamy situation, that makes so much more *rational* sense than celebrating the emaciated figures of those who appear half-starved, was actually happening in my very own community. Had we taken the opportunity to compare notes as teens, we each would have had just a little more evidence, a few more tools and a wee bit more sane wisdom with which to navigate the culture's obsession with appearances.

Dark sisters and light ones need to get together and listen to one another's stories. Latina sisters need to fess up to Asian ones. Able-bodied women need to sit down with sisters who live with disabilities. And are you ready to hear about the marginalized group you never even knew existed? The beautiful ones. Really, it's true. In the last month I've met three drop-dead gorgeous sisters—one black, one white and one of mixed race—who each have a heart for other women to be set free from our culture's enslavement to physical perfection. One is a former model, one was a cheerleader for the Dallas Cowboys, and the other is a radiant young mother. These beautiful women confided in plain old me that because they are, in the humble words of one, "non-ugly," not a lot of folks will give them the time of day. Most tend to discount anything they have to say about beauty because these women don't know what it's like to be average. Other women avoid them, and guys are scared of them. Perhaps you never even knew that sad stuff. My point here is that as we build bridges with other women, across all kinds of unspoken barriers, we dispel the lies that keep us all bound.

The greatest weapon against lies is truth. So keep it real, sister.

26

FRIENDSHIP

I Get By with a Little Help from My Friends

As it was in my childhood, big-box discount clothing retailers are still among the most treacherous places I can imagine.

For new reasons.

Now, I *love* them! In recent years I would drive past Marshalls on the way to therapy, glancing at my watch to see if I could fit in a quick stop. Every week I was driven by the desperate worry: *What if they've got something fantastic in there right now, possibly lime green with cute polka dots, that I don't even* know *about?!?* I was the proverbial Pavlovian dog, salivating and responding on cue, to the bold graphic logo for Marshalls, Target and T.J.Maxx. I wanted to live differently, but I kept getting sucked into the consumer vacuum of automatic-opening doors. Of course, I wasn't alone. What was unique about my particular predicament, though, was the whole vocation situation: you know, the one in which I exhort other women to live differently, to make better choices. Nice, huh?

Hear me: when I've spoken to audiences, I've never acted as if I *weren't* in the same boat as every other woman. Of course I was. I didn't pretend like I never darkened the doors of one of these joints. Rather, I was able to say, "I, too, have been tempted. In fact, every Tuesday morning at 9:47." It would have been great if I'd had my act completely together, but I just didn't. Still don't.

Here's an example, from a family beach vacation, of me not having my act together. For the record, *vacation* means the week of the year in which I usually try to knock off most of the seven deadly sins. This particular year was no exception. Although my sister-in-law and I had honestly left the house with every intention of buying *groceries*, we somehow ended up at T.J.Maxx. I believe it was under the guise of buying a birthday present for her husband—since we were all about honoring the husband. We'd been frantically shopping for a while, for ourselves, by the time we got to beachwear. I was clutching several pairs of fantastic polka-dot surfer shorts in assorted colors. Not only do I not surf, but the store didn't even carry a size to fit me. Quite possibly the manufacturer did not make one. In my mind, though, I whipped up a quick plan to lose enough weight by the following summer to fit into them. I really do love polka dots *that* much.

Suddenly, I heard a woman across the aisle say, "Margot?"

I glanced up to see who was saying my name in a random, out-of-state beach location. Though I didn't quite recognize her, she explained, "You led our women's retreat at Windy Gap." Of course I did. That would be the retreat where I had poked fun at T.J.Maxx, and at myself, and had exhorted us all toward a higher road. Priceless. Really, you can't make this stuff up.

Feeling red-faced and quickly surveying what I had in my clenched fists, I tried to act warm and natural. As we chatted, though, my mind raced like an addict caught in a crack house. *There's nothing wrong with just being here,* I rationalized. *There may be something just a little bit off about buying these shorts I can't fit into,* I admitted silently to just myself. *But she doesn't know I can't squeeze my butt into them.* And on it went. Clearly, I was less than present to the unexpected meeting.

When I reported this funny thing to my husband, he laughed and suggested it was like a preacher being caught by a parishioner in a strip club. The funny part there, of course, is that the pastor and the parishioner are both at a strip club, right? Funny in a sad way, I mean. This, I reasoned, was kind of the women's version of that. Or rather, it *would* have been like that—except for the fact that Christine and her kids had actually been outside at the sandy beach preparing for a family mission trip to Appalachia when a sudden rainstorm came up and they had to find shelter in the T.J.Maxx.

Like I said, you can't make this stuff up.

Although it wasn't my finest moment, I am real clear that I need friends—and strangers—like this to keep me on track.

HAIR BUDDY

At that same women's weekend in beautiful Windy Gap, North Carolina, I had blathered on about all the crazy things we women do to make ourselves appear acceptable to others when, in Christ, we are already altogether accepted. We are, people, we really are.

At the end of the weekend, the planning team was wrapping up power cords and straightening up the skit closet when my new friend Dana shared with me her new resolve. She wanted to let me know that, upon returning home, she had plans to march right over to her hairdresser and break up with her. (Her words, not mine.) There was also some chatter about recent $150 highlights that—in my opinion—weren't actually visible to the naked eye. Dana was going to let her hairdresser know that she wouldn't be darkening the salon doors for a while.

For this to succeed, I knew Dana needed support. I did too. That's why, as she finished wrapping up power cords, Dana and I decided to become hair buddies. A hair buddy is sort of like a twelve-step group sponsor. She is someone you can call when roots get dark and resolve gets dicey.

Anyone who knows me is surely wondering why I would need someone to talk me down from hair improvement since, well . . . since I look like I do. Here's my true confession: I love being a summer blondie. I do. At the women's weekend I had explained to over two hundred women, my brown roots exposed, how fourteen months earlier I had used half a bottle of Sun-In and had come home from the family beach vacation looking all glimmery. I *loved* that yellow hair. Even a few of the gentlemen at church had let me know how great I looked.

Here's the rub, though. Not long after I'd gone golden, I was sitting next to my daughter and chatting with her while she got a haircut. Faced with a huge, imperfection-enhancing mirror, I asked her my usual question, with a little twist: "If there was one thing *you* could change about you, what would it be?"

Without missing a beat, my beautiful little brunette answered, "I'd make my hair yellow. Or black."

Never before had she ever come up with anything. I was devastated. Do you see it? I had *elicited* her discontent. I had *done* that weird thing to her. When I was entirely happy with my natural self, she was too. Then I make myself look a little more golden, a little shinier, and she decides that she'd like to change herself up too.

I know that not everyone thinks this is a big deal. Some of you may even think it's fantastic. Not me. In fact, I was pretty sad at that dissatisfied announcement. It was a powerful lesson for this mama. And although I had told all the women gathered for the weekend that I was swearing off hair-coloring, I still knew it would be hard to keep my hands off the bleach. So it was nice to go home knowing I had a hair buddy who would be there for me if I should be tempted to tint.

Then, not long before Christmas, I got this email from Dana: "Over Thanksgiving, my sister asked me, 'What is going on with your hair?' I defensively asked her, 'What do you mean?' She wanted to know if my hairdresser had died because it looks like I haven't seen her since June! I told her that actually it was August. My sister called me today and told me I really should go get my hair done. She reminded me I have a fancy Christmas party for my husband's office next week, and I have never met a lot of people from his company. Do I really want them to see me like this?"

Yes. Yes, hair buddy. Yes you do. It's exactly how you want them to see you.

I hope it's becoming alarmingly obvious that those who choose to navigate this precarious road shouldn't travel alone.

ENOUGH IS ENOUGH

I need help holding fast to my commitments on all sorts of fronts. A number of months ago I received an email from an old friend. In it Sarah explained that she'd recently decided to purge her home of unwanted clothing and other unused junk. "It was shameful," she confessed. "Talk about stuff! I kept thinking about Jesus' caution about not storing up treasures on earth. I made a personal commitment not to purchase any more clothing for my-self for one year! So far it feels kind of good . . . and freeing."

I was intrigued. After all, Sarah wasn't some communal-living Jesus hippie, like I want to be. She wasn't one of those ring-nosed, lock-haired radicals. Like I also want to be. Rather, my friend was a minivan-driving mom, living out what she thought was right.

Truth be told, Sarah was living the way I wanted to be living. Even before her email landed in my inbox, something in my gut— some would call it *conscience*—had already begun to tug. For months I'd been bothered by the obvious fact that although I had all the clothes I technically *needed*, and certainly more than I could cram into my drawers, I still kept buying more. I didn't do it in a clinically hoarding or compulsive way, just in the normal American way. I had been toying with this idea, about not buying clothes for a year, for a while. And, yes, I am aware that it's an absurdly weird privileged premise from the get-go. So occasionally, every few months, I'd think about it. But then I'd not think about it for several more months. Without Sarah's accidental intervention, I might have limped along like this for years.

Sensing that Sarah's weird spiritual discipline might have my name on it, I cautiously entertained the possibility of joining her. I thought about how grateful I'd been to have Dana as a hair buddy. *As far as spiritual practices go, it shouldn't be* that *hard,* I reasoned. *Technically, it's doing nothing.* After thinking about it for a day, I decided that I could probably do nothing. I anxiously replied to Sarah's email.

"I'm kind of nervous to say this," I wrote. "Okay, *really* nervous . . . I want to do this year with you. Can we be clothing buddies?" Then I quickly tapped "Send" before I could change my mind.

Sarah and I quickly discovered that although our wills were committed to the clothing fast, it would take a few weeks for our hearts and minds to catch up. It was like consumer detox. For instance, Sarah reported that while grocery shopping she'd been seized with the odd, overwhelming urge to buy colored tights. Since, barred from clothing stores, I'd recently coveted grocery store clothing myself, I completely understood.

Then the fashion troubles began. More so than usual, I mean. The fact that my undies ride a good four-and-a-half inches higher than my jeans, in the back, had never bothered me enough to take action. It had bothered me a tiny little bit but, like I said, not enough to do anything about it. Suddenly, when I couldn't buy clothes for twelve months, the situation felt absolutely critical—as in matter-of-national-security critical. But what could I do? The nation, I grudgingly decided, was just going to have to catch glimpses of my undies for twelve more months. Eventually, the roller-coaster ride of weird fantasies, bargaining and angst finally gave way to acceptance.

During our year as clothes buddies, there were plenty of garments that Sarah and I still *wanted.* Like raspberry-colored tights. We were both surprised, however, by how very few we actually *needed.* Sarah, who lives in northern New Jersey, was three months into our experiment when she reached her icy cold hands into her coat pockets to discover that she'd lost a glove. It was her first real need. Three months!

From the get-go, I decided to keep a running list of clothing I found I needed. That way, when the year was over, I could rush right out and go shopping, feeling sort of proud about how deprived I'd been. Besides the troubling Pantygate debacle, which doesn't quite meet Abraham Maslow's criteria for a critical physiological human need, the closest thing to a need that I could whip up was a light green T-shirt. I had a few sweaters and sweatshirts that would have worked great over a light green T-shirt, and I just didn't have one. Oh, sure: if I really knocked myself out I might have been able to make them work over the white, the black, the orange, the pink, the purple, the light blue, the brown or the kelly green. In a pinch. So, I suppose a light green shirt didn't technically qualify as a need. But I really *wanted* light green.

It was the closest thing I had to a need all year.

Top Ten Weird Excuses That Go Through My Mind About Why I Might Possibly Need to Buy Clothes the Year I Decide to Buy No Clothes

1. Wedding Emergency
"It would be disrespectful to wear just any old thing that I've got in my closet to this wedding. I would actually be honoring this family, loving people well, by buying something new."

2. Funeral Emergency
See #1. And add, "I really need something in a darker shade. If I wear the pink dress I have, it might appear as if I'm not grieving enough."

3. Medical Condition
"Those cutie green shoes look like they'd be therapeutic for my chronically injured feet. It would actually be irresponsible, and poor stewardship of my body, to not buy them."

4. Misguided Philanthropy

"The ad says that this company gives 5 percent of each sale to charity. I think that purchasing these shorts, at great cost to myself and my integrity, would benefit others. And I'm all about others."

5. Professional Situation

"As a public speaker, people are forced to look at me for minutes on end. If I am going to do my job well, if I am going to be able to put food on the table for my children, if I'm going to share the gospel, I better buy something new."

6. Unforeseen Opportunity

"When I swore off buying new clothes in September, I had no way of foreseeing that I'd be traveling to Italy this year. Which obviously demands a new wardrobe."

7. Can't-Miss Opportunity

"This polka-dot sweater looks like it was made for me. It is so perfectly me that it would almost be a slap in God's face to not buy it. It's so me."

8. Promises of Grandeur

"This display says that the product I am viewing is 'the ultimate tee.' Ultimate. If I have a chance to buy the 'ultimate tee,' it almost seems like I have to. Because it's the ultimate."

9. Nostalgic Honoring

"This dress looks just like the one my precious grandmother wore in 1940. Only a different length. And color. And style. It would honor her so much if I bought this one."

10. Seasonal Exception

"Obviously, there was no way I could have known that I'd find this to-die-for Halloween bracelet with ghosts and bats and witches. I feel certain this isn't covered under the original stop-shopping contract. Since I didn't know about this particular novelty bracelet."

OTHER EFFECTS

As a result of the clothing experiment, I slowly began to come to the dawning realization that a gracious Provider had already met *all* of my needs.

I even began to suspect that the desperation about all the stuff I wanted might have been artificially induced. That's not to say that my angst over the high-riding panties wasn't real. It most certainly was. But during the purchase-less year without new clothes, I stumbled upon a sociological theory. My theory suggests that groups tend to maintain a certain level of stress, even generating artificial stresses if the regular ones aren't enough. Though I'm not convinced that the studies had effectively re-searched the lasting ill effects of abstaining from lime green T-shirts, the idea still put a lot into perspective for me. When we don't live with the natural stresses of rival tribes running at us with spears, or the possibility of being killed by wild lions, or the pressures of hunting and gathering, or the dependence upon a fickle rain god to water our crops—well, we sort of whip up our own stressors.

So although the harvest is good, grocery shelves are stocked and our fridges are full, the fact that our roots are growing in dark can feel entirely critical to our survival. And though we have warm homes in which to live, we stress out about finding the place mats we saw in *Martha Stewart Living* magazine—the ones with a hand-stitched border that match the picture frames we al-ready have that coordinate with our fair-trade candles. So when we're out shopping and we see the perfect pair of shoes, we think that *finally* our lives might settle down a little, and that we might be able to relax and that we might live better if only we owned those shoes. This is what I'm saying about drumming up imagi-nary stressors in the absence of the natural ones.

I think this might explain why the situation with the high-riding panties felt so critical. Had I been scavenging through dumpsters to feed my children, I probably would have been perfectly fine with my panties. In the absence of that desperation, my needs well met, I had created my own weird stressor.

SHOELESSNESS

The same year, a friend sent me an online video featuring facts about shoes, which seemed to be part of some shoe-the-world campaign. As someone who blogs about shoes and other stuff, it seemed incumbent upon me to check it out. Here's what I learned.

Fact #1: In some developing nations, children must walk for miles for food, clean water and medical help.

Fact #2: Cuts and sores on feet can lead to serious infection.

Fact #3: Often, children cannot attend school barefoot.

Fact #4: In Ethiopia, approximately one million people are suffering from podoconiosis, a debilitating and disfiguring disease caused by walking barefoot in volcanic soil.

Fact #5: Podoconiosis is 100 percent preventable by wearing shoes.[1]

Like I said, the facts were forced upon me when I innocently clicked on a link my friend Rachel had sent me on Facebook. Apparently she, and thousands of others, planned to go shoeless for one day to raise awareness about how a pair of shoes can change a life.

Personally, I planned to show my support by posting a very enthusiastic blog entry and be done with it. I would be prayerful on shoeless Thursday, on behalf of the needy millions, but I'd still wear shoes. Of course I wouldn't sign up to register my support on the Facebook group because I knew, in my heart, that I'd be wearing shoes. No one likes a hypocrite.

SHOES, Margot?!?! How dare you! You can't act like you care about

---

[1]See <www.TOMSshoes.com>.

the shoeless and then wear SHOES on Thursday!

Believe me, the fact that shoefulness smacks a bit of podiatric hypocrisy is not lost on me.

Let me explain. In my mind, I'd gotten myself off the hook because I can't walk without shoes due to my chronically injured feet. I tiptoe a little without them, but I can't get farther than twenty or thirty feet. I certainly can't walk my kids to school, and I wasn't entirely sure if I could drive them. So I was feeling fine about being prayerfully shoed on Thursday, until I got this sweet note from Rachel: "Let's paint our toenails a fun color for Thursday." Somehow she mistakenly inferred from my bloggish enthusiasm that my actual *feet* would be participating in the event.

Not only was that pretty polish offer hard to resist, but the more I thought about it, I just wasn't so certain that I *wasn't* being called to identify with those less fortunate—who also can't walk without shoes—who weren't simply being inconvenienced for a single day. *Crabbily, I realized I couldn't not do it.*

Crabby reluctance is usually what following Jesus looks like for me.

On Shoeless Thursday, I got out of bed, told the kids to get moving as I limped past their rooms and hobbled downstairs, on my toes, to get grounded. On a normal morning, before I walk, I gingerly rest my socked, shoed feet on the floor at ninety degrees for ten minutes, in order to ground them with a gentle stretch.

Though I had imagined myself in some kind of Norman Rockwell scene, sitting at the kitchen table serenely spreading peanut butter and jelly onto bread, once I was up I pretty much just sat there and bossed my kids around to gather their breakfasts, lunches, shoes and backpacks.

The morning's unforeseen snafu was that my youngest son couldn't find his shoes. The irony wasn't lost on me. Nor was it even very unforeseen. It happens all the time. On the upside, it's because each boy owns only one pair of shoes which fits. So there's something of which to take note on a day when the over-shoed remember the needy. On the downside, though, I can get really ugly when the boys can't find their shoes. When I'm shoe-less, apparently, I get even meaner.

"You go through every room in this house until you find those shoes," I hissed. As is his way, he wandered around a little bit and then ended up wrestling with his brother.

"Mom," he whined, "I can't find my shoes."

"Find them," I roared through gritted teeth.

Hobbling to the living room and falling into a comfortable chair, I reached my right hand under the chair, like one of those arcade games with the claw, and wrapped my hand around a small shoe. And then another. Though he never admitted it, I sus-pect my son had shoved them under the skirted chair when I'd asked him to put them away after changing into cleats—yes, we do own specialty shoes—for soccer practice the previous evening. The instruction, of course, had been issued so that he could find them in the morning.

Yet another bitter irony.

After driving the kids to school—which, despite the metal pedals, is actually easier than walking—I did not move from my chair more than once or twice until I picked the kids up from school six-and-a-half hours later.

I would never have gotten into this mess, of course, if it hadn't been for my sweet, good-hearted, polished-toed friend. *I think this is always the way with discipleship. It's supposed to be lived out in com-munity. Believe me, without my faithful friends, I'd be* much *more com-fortable than I already am.*

So if you bump into me at Target or Walmart, please feel free to peek in my basket. And be prepared to ask some questions.

27

PRACTICES

The Next Thing

I realize that, just possibly, I get a little too jazzed about this stuff. I do. I get all fired up about those of us who belong to Jesus responding to his invitation to live differently. I'm much more excitable than most when it comes to buying fewer clothes, loving my curvy hips and living with my natural hair color. I welcome you to check back in with me in a few years, once my pigment is entirely spent; I'm entirely willing to entertain the possibility that I may be singing a different tune.

A few years ago I was teaching a Sunday school class about the zillions of ways that we could all live differently by embracing a kingdom vision of justice, love and fresh spiritual practices that involve high-riding panties. In hindsight, I suspect it must have been just exhausting to sit there and have to listen to it all. Afterward, a woman who hadn't said a lot during the class came up to speak to me as everyone was leaving.

Quietly and sincerely, she shared, "I've realized that I don't have to do *everything*, just the *next* thing."

Isn't that the most insightful remark you've heard in your entire life?! It was *way* better than anything I had come up with. Today I always try to include it whenever I enumerate a big long list of a gazillion things we could all be doing differently if we really put our minds to it.

Just do the *next* thing.

MY NEXT

I'd known now for about three days what my "next thing" had to be.

That's because three days ago, having grudgingly chauffeured my offspring to a local swimming pool, I realized that the reason I don't jump off of diving boards anymore is because I don't want a captive audience watching everything jiggle. I have to suspect that there are more than a few other landlubbing women in that same docked boat with me. So how sad is it that I, and other hot, sweaty, self-conscious women, are sitting ten feet from a cool body of water, while less self-conscious humans are bouncing and splashing and frolicking?! If I was going to put my money where my mouth was on all this body image nonsense, however, I suddenly knew that I had to jump off that board.

Today was the day.

Hobbling barefooted over to the board and placing my glasses safely under it, I climbed up the ladder and headed for the board's bouncy end. I faltered a little on my approach. I think it's because my naked feet just aren't used to being walked on, let alone choreographing anything that's going to precede a big splash. So I backed up, tried again and jumped as high as I could before diving headfirst into the water. Mission accomplished!

After diving in, I swam over to my waiting kiddos to check in with them. In hindsight, I don't know why I had to confirm what I already knew, but for some reason I did it anyway.

Popping my head out of the water, I queried, "Did everything shake?"

"Yes," Zoë confirmed, wise enough not to go into too much more detail.

Then my honest eight-year-old son Rollie added, "It always does."

I am so not inviting him to whatever the next weird thing is.

MADE FOR MORE

I've become convinced that discipleship, following Jesus, is *all about* the next thing. Because we were made to love God and others, Jesus sets us free from a death-dealing preoccupation with self so that we can be *with* others and *for* others. Even if those others do tell us the ugly truth about how our bodies jiggle.

Here's the real beauty of the plan: you don't have to wait until you get your naturally self-referenced act together to move toward a new way of living. Great news, huh? In fact, the choice to take the baby steps is what actually *pulls* us outside of our constraining and exhausting self-referenced bind. Like I said, it's a great setup.

For instance, you don't need to overhaul your entire diet, eating only food grown and raised on your porch, before taking a baby step like redirecting your weekly gourmet coffee budget toward sponsoring a child through Compassion International.

You don't need to wear an itchy burlap-sack wardrobe before taking the small step to buy clothes, even yummy ones with a bit of flair, just when you actually *need* them.

You don't need to hike seven miles to the grocery store to pick up a quart of milk before trying out a smaller step, such as coordinating all your vehicle-propelled shopping to happen on just one day a week.

Getting serious about living into God's good intentions for these bodies doesn't even mean that you can never look extra-fruity delicious in lime green again. (What a relief, right?) It's not about looking *bad*. Instead, the movement into which God is gently calling us is to lift our eyes from our own navels (or noses or hips or thighs) in order to turn our gaze toward others.

YOUR NEXT

Clearly, that smartie Sunday school student was right. We're not asked to do *everything*. We're simply invited to tag along with Jesus and to follow him into the *next* thing. I don't presume to know what your next thing might be. Whether it's something that happens at a crowded swimming pool, or whether it's skipping a hair appointment, or whether it's trimming out the Ben & Jerry's, or whether it's just deciding to be satisfied with your body—my prayer for you is that you say "yes."

Of course enlightened women like us *know* better. Jesus invites us to *live* better.

WHAT'S THE NEXT STEP?

Here's what's next: get yourself a *Body Buddy*. Find a friend with whom you can walk in this new life-giving way. Agree with one another that bodies are made for relationship with others and dream of what life might be like if you lived into that reality together. Then . . . live it.

Here a few ideas for possible first steps . . .

1. *Refrain from Negative Comments*
   Commit to refraining from making any negative comments about your body: hair, butt, skin, thighs, stomach, the whole works. (I hope it goes without saying that you won't be making negative comments about other women's bodies . . .)

2. *Drink Fairly Traded Coffee*
   Since I'm not a coffee drinker, I can't presume to recommend kicking the coffee habit—even though that's exactly what I'm thinking—but I can suggest committing to consume only coffee that has been fairly traded. Read Julie Clawson's Everyday Justice *to learn more. (And then get your church on board!)*

3. Fast from Soda

Really, can you even come up with two good reasons to drink that stuff? Or even one that's not about your personal enjoyment? Why not take a soda break for a few months and journal about the process. (Using your leftover soda money to supply clean drinking water to those in need wouldn't hurt either.)

4. Walk to Accomplish Your Business

Are there any errands you regularly drive to within a mile of your home? Walk them! If you can buy a gallon of milk, check out a library book, rent a video or purchase stamps, walk it.

5. Eliminate Harmful Media

Imagine what life would be like if you weren't being bombarded by the constant pressure, in the media, to be physically attractive. A better world is possible. Consider canceling a magazine subscription or cutting out television for a while. You may be amazed.

6. Use Your Body to Sustain Life

Okay, you don't have to pull out the back-breaking washing board to clean your clothes, but consider how you might use your body to participate in the work needed to sustain your bodily life. Wash some dishes. Iron a shirt. Grow tomatoes. Cook some applesauce. Be reminded of what bodies are for. (And share the tomatoes and applesauce with your neighbors.)

7. Clothe Yourself Responsibly

When you actually need clothes or shoes, try a thrift shop. Or buy used on eBay. You and your Body Buddy could host a Clothing Swap, where all your friends bring the clothes they're no longer using and trade out for fresh ones. (This really is fabulously fun!) Why bring new clothes into the world when there are already so many that need good homes?

8. Bend to Do Garbage Squats

Invite your Body Buddy to go on a trash walk with you. Choose the messiest neighborhood you can think of and bend at the knees to pick up their garbage.

9. Freeze Your Shoe-Buying

Inventory the shoes in your closet. That, in itself, should be life-changing. If you've got what you need, though, commit to not buying new shoes until your old ones are no longer wearable. (The more horrible that sounds to you means it is probably all the more likely to benefit you. And others.)

10. Walk and Talk with Your Body Buddy

Commit to joining your Body Buddy for a walk each week. If you're limited physically, meet to share a cup of yummy fairly traded coffee. Share with one another how your commitment to use your bodies for the purpose for which they were made is going. When I did this with a friend, the first time I sort of sugar-coated the reality of the daily nitty-gritty. Then when she came clean about her struggles, I could more easily see the areas where I was really struggling. Confession is the best thing going. Use it responsibly.

EPILOGUE

Sermon on a
Twenty-First-Century Mount

If I had a mountain, and a crowd of twenty-first-century women, this is what I'd want them to hear:

Blessed are those who aren't fantastically attractive, because they have a treasure that's found elsewhere.

Blessed are those who grieve the loss of their youthful beauty, for they will be comforted.

Blessed are those who are overlooked at a singles bar, for they are actually the ones chosen to receive an even greater blessing.

Blessed are those who hunger and thirst for something more than physical beauty, for they will be filled with what really satisfies.

Blessed are those whose merciful eyes search for the best in others, for they will receive mercy.

Blessed are those whose hearts are pure, for they will see God and recognize his holy imprint on the ones he's made.

Blessed are those who use their bodies to work for peace, for they will be called God's own.

Blessed are those who suffer, socially or emotionally or physically, because they have made some of these choices, for they have a better reward coming.

Let me break it down. You weren't made to be *viewed*. That's like popping a bowl of yummy popcorn and then just *looking* at the salt sitting on the shelf instead of sprinkling it on top. Like salt, you were made for a *purpose*. With your *body*, you were made to be *for* others.

You're also sort of like a keychain flashlight. Its purpose isn't to draw attention to itself, to its shiny plastic shell or silver beady cord. A light is made to give light to *others!* (Like the ones who can't find their keys in their big messy purses or the ones who just can't see where they're going at night.) You're the kind of light that's supposed to illumine the face of your Father in heaven, so that others will see him more clearly, in your actual countenance.

In Jesus' coming, he fulfilled the law. In him we see what it really means to live.

For instance, you already know not to murder, but don't even do it with your tongue. Use your body to bless people, not curse them. If you have blown it, which you probably will, do what it takes to be reconciled.

You know not to sleep around with other people's husbands, like Angelina Jolie's, but don't even daydream about it. Don't use your eyes to devour juicy tabloids or semi-pornographic romance novels.

If you're divorced, don't give your body, intimately, to others.

Be a person who keeps your commitments. Be someone who's known for her "yes" meaning "yes" and her "no" meaning "no." Don't "swear by your head," for you cannot make even one hair white or black. (Well, technically you can, but you can't choose the color of those roots when they grow back in!)

You've seen catfights in which women grab one another by the hair and claw at each other with pretty fingernails. Whether or not we do it in a parking lot or do it in our hearts, that's kind of how we're wired. But I say to you, if someone steals your parking space, hop out and open the door for her. If she slept with your husband before you were married, treat her with dignity. If she did it after you were married, same deal.

Seriously, outdo your enemies with kindness. Pray for them, because you're both going to need it. If you just love those warm fuzzy friends who take you out for coffee and cake on your birthday every year, what good is that? Anyone can do that. If you're plowing your way through Costco and only grin at the folks you know from church, what use is that? Even the Wiccan Neo-Pagans do that. The real way to greatness is to strive to be like my Dad.

Don't waste your energy and time and money drawing attention to yourself, to your worthiness. The kind of attention you'll get isn't worth much anyway. When you give to others, and when you pray and when you fast, enjoy the approving gaze of our Father, who always takes notice of what's done quietly, for him.

Although it's completely natural to want to gather clothes, shoes, makeup and other fun stuff, be careful. That's where your heart will end up. It's just the way things work. I'm not saying it wouldn't be great to invest in all that stuff *and* serve God too. It would. It just doesn't work that way.

You want to invest in what really counts? Make your *eyes* beautiful. They're the lamp of the body. You *really* shine not when others are gawking at you, but when the light that's in you shines upon others. You can do that—shower others with light—with your actual eyes!

It's natural to get caught up with calories and outfits. I get that. But there's more to life than food and clothes. Maybe you don't realize how incredibly precious and valuable you are to your Father. He's *already* concerned that you get what you need—even if he doesn't place a particular priority on designer jeans or Slim-

Fast shakes. Think about it: the birds don't waste any energy stockpiling canned goods in their pantries, and God feeds them. In fact, check out the colors the lilies are wearing! If God has clothed them so beautifully, don't you think he'll meet your needs? When you take your mind off of all the stuff the world scrambles after, and set it on our Father's kingdom, I think you'll be surprised how you find your needs met.

RESOURCES

Check out this list of resources for the journey.

WEBSITES

www.TrueCampaign.com
Challenging the culture's ideas about identity and beauty.

http://truecampaign.org/trueshift
The "true:shift" campaign is the True Campaign's dynamic partnership with Food for the Hungry.

www.youtube.com/watch?v=iYhCn0jf46U
You've got to see this billboard model get made over.

www.FindingBalance.com
Resources and support for those with eating and body issues, particularly those not otherwise specified.

www.StoryofStuff.com
This takes twenty minutes, and you'll never look at buying stuff the same way again.

www.BetterWorldShopper.com
This little guide has done all the legwork for those who want to buy clothes, food, gas and more produced justly.

www.TOMSshoes.com
TOMS donates one pair of shoes for every one sold.

www.Compassion.com
Your monthly sponsorship releases a child from poverty in Jesus' name. You can *do* this.

www.WorldVision.org
Apply your resources to end sex trafficking of women and children.

www.IJM.org
Learn more about International Justice Mission and how you can participate in the liberation of the bodies God loves.

www.willowcreek.org/coh
Check out Willow Creek's Celebration of Hope challenge and learn what the world's poor eat.

www.OperationBeautiful.com
Women leave Post-it notes of encouragement and support for one another in random places like bookstores and public restrooms.

www.RemudaRanch.com
Remuda Ranch offers treatment for women and girls suffering from eating disorders.

GROUP DISCUSSION QUESTIONS

A word to group leaders about discussion questions . . .

Two words really: *no sweat*. These questions are provided as a springboard for you to discuss what's in your heads and hearts. You'll know it's going well when women get past the stuff we usually talk about—bad hair, big butts, baby bellies—and reveal what's really happening in their heads and hearts. Be sure to explain up front that your group is a safe space. What's shared in the circle, *stays* in the circle.

INTRODUCTION

1. Describe and discuss pop culture's portrayal of the physically ideal woman. How do you measure up to that image? Do you try?

2. What are some of the ways that women of various ethnicities feel the pressure to fit the world's mold of beauty?

3. According to Jesus, the blessed woman is one who responds

to God's voice. Can you fill out a more detailed picture of a woman like this? Do you know one?

PART ONE: THE PROBLEM

1. If you could change one thing about your body, what would it be?

2. Do you watch any reality makeover shows? Do you find them helpful or harmful? How so?

3. Which current advertisements offer to fix something that's wrong about your body? Is it a condition that's really *so* wrong?

4. What are you tempted to turn toward to soothe your anxiety (e.g., food, drink, spending, etc.)? What might it look like for you to "trust in what the Father provides"?

5. For what sorts of qualities are you tempted to pre-judge other women (e.g., race, shape, dress, culture, education, etc.)? How have you been able to put the brakes on this temptation?

6. How difficult is it for you to stop consuming (such as food, clothes, etc.) once your needs have been met? Do you have any ideas why?

7. How are women in this culture *thingified*? What are some ways that we can "step off the court"?

8. In what types of situations are you tempted to give *lots* of attention to yourself and your appearance (such as work, church, visits home, etc.)? Is there another type of situation in which you forget yourself entirely to focus on another?

PART TWO: THE PURPOSE

9. Does your faith community talk about beauty or body image? What's the message you hear? Is there an unspoken message?

10. According to the world's values, are types of women undervalued? Are kingdom priorities different? How?

11. What do you think about the idea Margot mentions that people were made unique in order to be *recognized*? Do you agree with it? How do you think others recognize you?

12. In what situations do you feel like your physical body is doing exactly the thing it was made to do?

13. Are there garments or accessories or colors that make you feel like the beloved woman you were made to be?

14. Can you list some of the many ways that your needs—for food, clothing, shelter, relationship—are being sufficiently met?

15. Which shaming lies that insist that you're not acceptable are you quick to believe? What truths might God use to replace them?

16. Christians are to be *marked* by love. Can you think of some fresh ways in which a body might be visibly marked by love?

17. Are you naturally touchy or more naturally private? Are there ways you are being called to extend physical affection to others?

18. Is there a way in which you respond to God by loving *others* with your body? For instance, is there a *particular* way God has called you to care for others?

PART THREE: THE PLAN

19. Can you picture a human face that has looked on you with unconditional love and affection? Whose?

20. Can you think of fresh ways in which followers of Jesus can pattern our bodily lives after his? What does it look like to imitate Jesus, with our bodies, in the twenty-first century?

21. What kinds of opportunities do you have—or *make*—to use your body to meet your needs and those of others?

22. How hard do you resist—or plan to resist—physical signs of aging? What qualities do you admire in women who are "aging gracefully"?

23. Are there any helpful ways you've discovered to responsibly manage your consumption of food? In what situations is it most difficult for you to eat in moderation?

24. Are there particular ways in which you try to make responsible clothing purchases? Do you feel like you're being a faithful steward in the ways you clothe yourself?

25. Is it tempting for you to draw attention to your body's imperfections? How do you feel when others ramble on about theirs?

26. How do—or how can—you and your friends support one another in the journey toward freedom from self-preoccupation? Can you think of any *practical* steps?

27. Margot says that on this journey into freedom, God only asks us to do the *next* thing. What might your next thing be?

Margot Starbuck now makes a concerted effort not to look too casually fantastic. This will become immediately evident should you ever meet her in person. Freed up from pouring a lot of time and energy into hair and makeup, and convinced that God liberates us to live a life of love that is for others, Margot helps readers and audiences make other creative leaps of discipleship in their own lives. She enjoys helping other women keep it real as one voice in the True Campaign's True Sisterhood. Margot lives in the Walltown neighborhood of Durham, North Carolina, with her husband and three yummy children. She loves hanging out at Reality Ministries—where she's embraced by friends with and without disabilities—because it's just the kind of scrumtrilescent marginless kingdom Jesus ushered in.

**Connect with Margot on Facebook
or learn more at www.MargotStarbuck.com.**

identity · beauty · influence

The True Campaign exists to end the crisis of
distorted self-image among women by challenging
cultural ideals about identity and beauty so we
can influence our world as God intended.